Breaking Kids Free From Screen Addiction

Restoring Children's Mental Well-Being in the Digital Age

Richard Bass

2 FREE Bonuses!

Receive a FREE <u>Planner for Kids</u> and a copy of the <u>Positive Discipline Playbook</u> by scanning below!

Table of Contents

Introduction

It has become appallingly obvious that our technology has exceeded our humanity. —Albert Einstein

The Great Disconnect

The invention of technology is a historical milestone in human evolution. The idea that you can communicate with and see people while being miles apart has transformed the way we access information, perform our work duties, source entertainment, and build and maintain relationships. As convenient as technology has been, it has also required us to develop new skills such as self-regulation. With self-regulation, we can manage how much space and time technology takes in our lives and implement the necessary boundaries to ensure a healthy balance of online and offline activities. On paper, this may sound easy to practice, but in reality, it takes a lot of self-control—something that a growing child simply doesn't have yet.

You may be capable of turning off the TV and sitting in silence or of going days without checking your social media or emails. When you are bored, you may be able to control the urge to pick up your phone and scroll through endless amounts of online content. However, your child may struggle to display the same level of self-control—not because they are weak, but because they are a child and still need guidance on how to manage technology.

Without your parental involvement, it's possible for technology to become the center of your child's life—something that they cannot separate themselves from. The appeal of technology for younger generations has a lot to do with how easily accessible and convenient it is. For instance, why would a toddler choose to play with a nonverbal toy when they can watch the animated toy come to life on the TV screen? Why would a young boy choose to ride his skateboard outside when he can practice riding it on a video game? And why would a teenager make the effort of planning face-to-face meetups with friends when they could engage on a group chat online?

A lack in technology restrictions and boundaries can lead to a great disconnect between you and your child, which will only get worse over the years as they gain independence and newer electronic devices hit the market. Furthermore, your child's growing dependency on electronic devices can change the nature of your parenting and threaten your sense of authority. Nowadays, it isn't strange for devices like TVs, tablets, computers, and cell phones to replace parents as the primary caretakers of children, impacting what children learn, behave, and develop. Imagine for a second that your toddler pays more attention to their cartoons over your instructions, or that your teen is more influenced by the content they view on social media than the wise counsel you seek to give them. Competing with electronic devices for your child's respect and obedience is something that you wouldn't want as a parent. So, why allow these devices to have such a stronghold on your child's daily life? Why not make the necessary changes to review and set limits on how much technology your child accesses at home?

Case Studies of Technology Addiction

There are countless stories detailing the negative impact of excessive screen time on children's cognitive, social, and emotional development. What's frightening is that more and more children are becoming addicted to technology. The term "technology addiction" is used loosely in this book to describe the impulsive and almost obsessive use of electronic devices, despite the negative consequences affecting the user (Robinson, 2024).

Have you heard of the zombie effect that occurs after several hours of uninterrupted screen time? Children become so fixated on the program or content they are viewing to the extent that they enter a trance-like state where they are incapable of unplugging or shifting their focus on something else. As such, they may struggle to pay attention, hold conversations, or follow instructions.

The zombie effect can also lead to developmental and behavioral issues. Take young Jack, a 3-year-old who spends more than 2 hours a day watching cartoons on a tablet. His parents have noticed that he becomes irritable and sometimes throws tantrums when the tablet is taken away. Moreover, he has fallen behind on his speech and language milestones due to not getting enough practice communicating with others. Emma, a bright 10-year-old girl, spends most of her free time at home playing video games.

Her parents have noticed a delay in executive function skills like attention, memory, planning, and problem-solving, which are normally built through active learning, critical thinking, and imaginative play. Subsequently, her grades have also taken a knock due to her underdeveloped executive function skills and her trouble with self-regulating.

Then there is Lucas, a 15-year-old teenage boy who is constantly on his phone. While having a phone has been useful when completing homework or staying in touch with family, Lucas stays active on social media throughout the day and night, leading to chronic sleep deprivation. This pattern of behavior has made Lucas withdrawn and anxious, particularly when dealing with social situations like asking for help at a store, making friends at school, or recognizing and responding to social cues.

Taking a Stand on Technology Addiction

Acknowledging technology addiction is something that you may shy away from due to the negative connotations surrounding the term. When you think of an addict, you might imagine someone whose life is in shambles as a result of their lack of self-control. However, looking at your child, you may notice signs of impulsive and obsessive use of technology and downplay it as a natural response to the tech-driven culture we live in rather than a harmful habit that your child has learned over the years.

Indeed, you cannot restrict your child from using technology, since the future is digital. However, you can restructure the relationship your child has with technology through implementing boundaries, encouraging mindful scrolling and social media use, and creating healthy routines that help your child strike a balance between online and offline activities.

You don't need to wait until you start noticing cognitive or social problems to take a stand on technology addiction, either. As the saying goes, preventing issues is better than medicating them. The only motivation you need to get started is to envision the type of adult you desire your child become.

To raise a conscious, self-disciplined, emotionally regulated, and confident child, they need to be curious about the world, possess a thirst for knowledge, and be exposed to other sources of information besides Google or ChatGPT. These qualities are developed through consistent parental monitoring and engagement, as well as by cultivating a household environment that promotes screen-free play and learning.

The Purpose of the Book

This book does not seek to bash technology or promote a technology-free lifestyle. However, it does seek to raise awareness to the growing problem of technology addiction among children and adolescents, and the devastating consequences it brings.

More importantly, the book takes a closer look at the relationship between excessive screen time and mental health disorders like anxiety, depression, attention-deficit hyperactive disorder (ADHD), and oppositional defiant disorder (ODD). It is not uncommon for young children to exhibit anxiety, depression, ADHD, or ODD symptoms when religiously glued to their screens. This has to do with the cognitive and social challenges caused by engaging with too much technology. Of course, this is not to say that excessive screen time leads to developing disorders like ADHD, as researchers have proven otherwise (Nguyen, 2023).

However, for children who are predisposed to various mental illnesses due to their genetics, medical history, or environment, being hooked on electronic devices can trigger or worsen mental health issues.

Beyond exploring the dangers of too much screen time, this book will also equip you with the tools and strategies to manage your child's technology usage at different ages. The younger the child, the more limits and rules you need to enforce to ensure that screen time doesn't impede their cognitive and social development. Older children can enjoy greater freedoms when using technology—however, your supervision and guidance is still required. The aim of the tools and strategies discussed in this book is to help you, the parent, regain a sense of control over how technology is integrated into your family life.

The Structure of the Book

To cover all aspects of technology usage, this book has been divided into five parts, namely:

- **Part 1—The Cognitive Effects of Excessive Technology Consumption:** Focuses on the scientific explanations of how screen time affects your child's cognitive development and discusses themes like attention span, learning challenges, and brain development.

- **Part 2—The Psychological Implications of Excessive Technology Usage:** Explores the impact of excessive screen time on your child's self-concept, self-esteem, and interpersonal behaviors.

- **Part 3—Preventative Measures for Technology Usage:** Provides strategies to address technology usage before dependency occurs. Strategies that are mentioned include setting boundaries, establishing healthy routines that limit screen time, and getting the whole family involved.

- **Part 4—Age-Specific Strategies for Cutting Back on Screen Time:** Offers tailored strategies for reducing screen time and encouraging more screen-free activities. These strategies have been grouped in different age groups: toddlers (0–2 years), preschoolers (3–5 years), elementary school children (6–12 years), and teenagers (13–18 years).

- **Part 5—Interactive Activities and Worksheets:** Provides practical tools such as activity ideas, sample schedules, and worksheets that can help you develop a structured approach to managing technology usage in your household.

You are welcome to go through the parts in no particular order and continuously refer back to the sections that you need. Note that some ideas expressed in the book may not be relevant to your child due to their age or personality. You have a unique style of parenting and will therefore find some strategies useful, and others, not so much. Remember that these are general suggestions that can be adapted to suit your child's needs and your family context.

Ultimately, the goal of this book is to support you in reclaiming your child's well-being so they can develop a healthier relationship with technology!

Part 1:

The Cognitive Effects of

Excessive Technology

Consumption

Chapter 1:

The Science Behind Screen Addiction

Technology is a useful servant but a dangerous master. —Christian Lous Lange

Brain Development and Screen Time

There are two important brain development stages that occur in a child's life. The first happens between the ages of two and seven, and the second during adolescence (Sriram, 2020). The information processed by your child during these critical stages helps their brain build solid neural connections, almost double the amount found in adult brains. What this means is that their brain acts as a sponge, practically absorbing anything and everything it is presented with. As such, your child's everyday experiences play a vital role in shaping how they think, feel, behave, and respond to their environment.

Offline creative and stimulating experiences like playing dress up, doing gardening, or playing sports strengthen your child's neural connections and provide opportunities for learning cognitive, social, and emotional skills. These skills are essential in cultivating identity formation, social awareness, and emotional intelligence.

Offline experiences can also expose your child to different social situations such as playing with other children, taking on different perspectives, empathizing with others, and resolving conflict through compromise. Through trial and error, they can eventually learn how to solve social problems and modify their behaviors according to various social expectations.

In contrast to this, online experiences like watching TV, playing games on the tablet, or scrolling through social media "numb" the parts of the brain that are crucial for learning, producing an underwhelming stimulation. There is not as much mental processing or problem-solving that your child can do while viewing online content, except forming opinions about what they are engaging with (i.e., whether the content is funny, sad, serious, entertaining, or boring).

Research from Common Sense Media shows that almost half of children aged 8 and below have a tablet device and spend an average of 2.25 hours a day on their screens (Cross, 2023). Imagine that during this time, their brains have gone to sleep. Over time, these children may experience delays in reaching their developmental milestones due to not building as many neural connections as a child who doesn't have a tablet and doesn't get as much screen time.

A 2023 study investigating the link between developmental growth and screen time found that one-year-old children who spent more than four hours per day on screens exhibited delays in speech and problem solving when they reached the ages of two and four.

Additionally, excessive screen time for one-year-old children was associated with delays to fine motor skills and social skills when they turned two (Takahashi et al., 2023). We can therefore safely say that unsupervised technology consumption can stunt the growth of young children and cause them to develop slower than their peers.

Some parents might assume that just because their children are watching educational content on their tablet or TV devices, learning is taking place. To some extent, children *do* learn by watching educational content online; however, constructive learning from screens only begins when children are between 36–42 months old (3–3.5 years old), and even so, in small and controlled amounts (Edmondson, 2018).

Offline learning is still the best way to keep a child under 3 years engaged and stimulated. Without the distraction of mind-numbing content, they can explore their surroundings, pick up on social cues from the children and adults around them, learn to recognize sounds and language, and get plenty of physical activity. Learning primarily offline means that, later on in life, they may have less trouble concentrating on tasks, thinking outside the box, and recognizing appropriate and inappropriate social behaviors.

Does Screen Type Matter?

You may be wondering if some electronic devices are better than others. Generally, all devices carry negative side effects. However, a study found that tablet users in particular suffered the most with brain function tasks like critical thinking and problem-solving. On the other hand, children who are heavy internet users or video gamers were found to have reduced brain volume and scored less on intelligence assessments than children who didn't engage with these types of media (Taylor & Francis, 2023). The type of content watched on screens has a great affect on your child's mental and emotional well-being. Generally, passive content that doesn't engage your child beyond moving their eyes carries little to no cognitive value. It is purely made for mindless consumption. Interactive content that seeks a response from your child, be it to move their body, solve a problem, sing along, or repeat a word, is considered high quality and can stimulate your child's brain. However, parental monitoring is still required to ensure that your child is engaging with the content.

Something else to consider is the pace of the shows and content that your child watches. Research shows that fast-paced content (i.e., content with rapidly moving frames and scenes) can overstimulate young children and cause executive function impairments, more specifically attention issues (Lillard & Peterson, 2011). This might lead to them being easily distracted while performing tasks or alternating between tasks without retaining focus and completing them. Slow-paced content encourages mindful viewing and assists children in learning new words, following the storyline, and reflecting on what they are hearing and watching.

Attention and Memory

Oftentimes, parents complain about their children's inability to hear them or take instructions when focused on their screens. Their kids develop what seems like "tunnel vision," where nothing else matters besides what they are viewing. But behind this frustrating habit lies deeper attention and memory issues that are caused by excessive technology usage. Executive function impairments are what contribute to the distractibility and lack of focus. The region of the brain known as the prefrontal cortex is responsible for developing executive function tasks like planning, organization, logical reasoning, problem-solving, goal-setting, and so on. Online experiences that do not stimulate the prefrontal cortex cause the region to temporarily shut down. In the long run, these crucial executive function tasks remain underdeveloped, creating social and academic challenges. It's worth mentioning that poor executive function skills is not the same as low intelligence. You can find bright children who thrive in sports, academics, or social situations but struggle to retain attention and memory, manage their time effectively, or stay organized. Furthermore, attention and memory issues are common for both children and adults, and shouldn't be seen as something that only happens with excessive screen time. For instance, it's normal for attention levels to fluctuate during the day, before or after meals, or when performing manual, repetitive tasks. Attention and memory issues could also be symptoms of developmental disorders like ADHD, autism spectrum disorder (ASD), or learning disabilities.

The Danger of Media Multitasking

Another factor to consider that might be worsening your child's attention and memory capabilities is the habit of multitasking, which is the practice of dividing your attention between more than one task at the same time. Media multitasking happens when your child switches between shows, channels, apps, or platforms without completing tasks. Older children might use more than one electronic device at the same time, such as watching a TV show while simultaneously browsing through social media on their cell phone.

Studies have found that media multitasking lowers attention span and the ability to focus on tasks until completion. It trains the brain to seek distractions so it can enjoy multiple forms of stimulation at the same time. Even when your child desires to focus on a task, their mind focuses on the next big thing, making whatever they are doing seem uninteresting or difficult. One of the ways that you can prevent media multitasking at home is to create a rule to turn off the TV during meal times, homework times, or when engaging in other household tasks. If your child wants to play music in the background, they should lower the volume enough to focus on their current task without getting distracted. Additionally, when your child is watching TV or playing video games, have them put their phone away. Encourage them to be fully present and engaged in their show.

Breaks in between technology use is also recommended. For example, after finishing an episode of a show, ask your child to stand up and complete an offline task before sitting down to start the next episode or engaging with another electronic device like working on their laptop. The best type of breaks involve going outside and getting some fresh air or taking a walk.

Excessive Screen Time vs. Screen Dependency vs. Screen Addiction

Throughout this chapter, we have used the term "excessive screen time" to explain the negative effects technology can have on children. However, what does excessive screen time mean and when does it reach the point of becoming a serious addiction? Excessive screen time is a general term to describe getting too much screen exposure, which can be anything above the age-appropriate guidelines outlined in the following section. For example, a 6-month-old baby watching more than 49 minutes of cartoons daily is getting too much screen time.

However, the problem gets more complicated when excessive screen time becomes a habit. Any behavior, good or bad, which is repeated consistently over time will eventually turn into a habit. To save time and energy processing the same input, the human brain learns to automatically carry out certain tasks at specific times. Signs that your child has developed a screen habit is that they perform certain screen-watching behaviors religiously. This could be tuning into their favorite shows at the same time each day or scrolling through the same social media apps, visiting the same websites, and doing so on an ongoing basis. The good news is that screen habits can be unlearned by introducing screen limits and other boundaries. The bad news is that unlearning screen habits gets tougher when your child has developed a screen dependency or addiction.

Screen dependency occurs when your child starts relying on screens to feel normal or calm, cure boredom, or entertain themselves. Without screens, they may feel physical pain or an inner void, as though something were missing. Think of how coffee drinkers depend on several cups of coffee to stay alert during the day. Their bodies have become accustomed to and reliant on caffeine to delay exhaustion. When they miss their first cup of coffee in the morning, they might experience muscle tension, mood swings, migraines, or trouble concentrating. Screen dependency has a similar effect on your child.

Screen addiction, on the other hand, can happen after several years of screen dependency. At this stage, your child may not be able to function without accessing their screens. It's also important to note that any addiction is considered a mental disease and therefore must be treated like one. Currently, there is no known cure for addiction, however treatment options such as abstinence, psychotherapy, rehabilitation programs, medication, support groups, and ongoing psychological evaluations are available.

Experts have found that addictions have a 40%–60% relapse rate, which means that falling back on unhealthy habits is common (Durning, n.d.). Recovery is a continuous journey that must be taken one day at a time. To prevent screen or technology addiction, take action by addressing unhealthy screen habits when they start to emerge. Act swiftly and immediately to avoid the stage where your child is dependent on screens to stay regulated during the day. Research has linked addiction to dopamine dysregulation, so balancing natural dopamine releases with screen-related dopamine releases is important (Sternlicht & Sternlicht, n.d.).

Teach your child to create their own fun instead of relying on their tablets, smartphones, or video games to provide entertainment. When they are young, encourage them to explore the garden, play dress up, or stimulate their mind with puzzles or board games. As they get older, enroll them into sports or social clubs that promote social and communication skills. These activities release dopamine but in small and sustainable amounts, unlike electronic devices that flood your child's brain with an abundance of dopamine.

The danger of excessive screen time is that your child may start to feel bored and unstimulated when carrying out everyday tasks that are healthy or compulsory, like going to school, completing homework, playing with their siblings, engaging in meaningful conversations with family, or getting sufficient physical exercise. Eventually, they may need excessive amounts of online activity and engagement to feel any sort of pleasure or normalcy.

More importantly, if your child has been diagnosed or shows signs of a mental health disorder like anxiety, depression, or ADHD, their dopamine production is significantly less compared to the average brain, which makes any kind of thrilling or pleasurable activity highly addictive (Sternlicht & Sternlicht, n.d.).

Children with ADHD in particular struggle with impulse control, which makes them vulnerable to screen dependency and addiction. Children with conditions like anxiety or depression may find solace in technology because it promotes social isolation, allowing them to hide behind screens and withdraw from people.

Age-Appropriate Guidelines

Now that you are aware of the cognitive dangers of excessive screen time, let's take a look at the table below that summarizes screen usage guidelines by age, as recommended by The American Academy of Child and Adolescent Psychiatry (2024).

The estimates mentioned in the table include the total time spent on online experiences across electronic devices. This includes time spent texting, watching videos on YouTube, listening to music or nursery rhymes, scrolling on social media, as well as time spent on other apps, conducting research, and doing homework. The reality is that many children are exceeding these estimates, spending hours online doing non-school-related activities. By using this table as your guide, you can help your child manage their time spent online more effectively.

Once again, it's worth emphasizing that screen time is not recommended for babies 18 months or younger. During this critical stage of their development, they should be busy on tasks and activities that allow them to engage their sense of touch, smell, sight, hearing, smell, and taste. They can learn more from playing with building blocks or running their hands through the mud than from mindlessly looking at a screen. On the rare occasions when exposing your child to screens, ensure that the content is slow, educational, and preferably something that you can watch together.

When regulating your child's screen time, consider the opportunity cost. Whenever possible, always choose offline activities as Plan A and screen-based activities as Plan B. For example, when your child is bored, irritable, or tired, take them outside to play an active game so they can run around and burn energy. If you want to keep them busy and stimulated indoors, take out art supplies and have them draw a picture or complete an age-appropriate craft activity.

Only when you have exhausted all of your offline activity ideas or run into uncontrollable factors like bad weather or lack of materials should you consider turning on the TV.

Throughout the book, you will be given more tips and strategies on how to manage your child's screen time to strike a good balance between online and offline activities.

Chapter 2

Technology and Mental Health

The real danger is not that computers will begin to think like men but that men will begin to think like computers. –Sydney J. Harris

How Screens Impact Your Child's Mental Health

In the previous chapter, we discussed the various ways that screen time can affect cognitive health, particularly in young children. We learned that children below three years old do not benefit from being exposed to electronic devices, even when the content is educational. At that tender age, their brains cannot process what they are viewing. Instead, giving children under three access to electronic devices inhibits their learning and can cause developmental delays. In this chapter, we are going to investigate the ways that excessive technology usage affects mental health.

The conditions that we will explore, such as overstimulation, anxiety, depression, ADHD, and ODD, become visible as children get older, even though the issues can be traced back to early childhood. The first step is for us to define mental health. According to the World Health Organization (WHO), mental health refers to the state and quality of your psychological well-being that enables you to function optimally as a human being (World Health Organization, n.d.). When your mental health is poor, you may find everyday tasks and routines to be tiresome and unfulfilling, whereas, when your mental health is in good shape, even the mundane moments of life feel meaningful.

When used excessively, technology can negatively impact your child's mental health. This has to do with the type and quality of media content viewed on electronic devices, as well as how often and for how long your child stays online. After a few hours, your child's brain experiences what is known as sensory overload or overstimulation as a result of not being able to process the sheer amount of information it is receiving at this fast pace. Imagine walking into an electronics shop and standing in front of 10 TVs framed on the wall, each one playing different types of content with different speeds, colors, and sound levels. Would you be able to keep up? Surely not.

Overstimulation is a clear warning sign that your eyes have been fixed on the TV for too long or that it's time to log out of your social media and take a moment to breathe and perform a slower and more relaxing physical task. The symptoms of overstimulation look similar to those activated when your child is stressed. They enter the fight-or-flight mode and either become extremely restless and agitated or appear "dazed" and emotionally withdrawn.

Other behaviors that your child could display include

- unexplained crying or whining

- lack of eye contact

- fatigue and sleepiness

- fidgeting and climbing on furniture

- physical aggression

- hyperactivity

- temper tantrums and irritability (particularly when they are interrupted)

Prolonged overstimulation can lead to chronic stress and serious mental health problems, which we will look at in the following sections. Bear in mind that most mental health issues are exacerbated by the overuse of technology, not caused by it. Therefore, children who are already at risk of learning and behavioral disorders due to past traumas, developmental delays, or hereditary illnesses need to be cautious of the amount of technology they consume, as this could worsen their preexisting symptoms or trigger dormant symptoms.

Anxiety & Depression

Anxiety and depression are two common types of mental health problems affecting children in the US. The 33rd Edition of the Kids Count Data Book found that 12% of children between the ages of 3 and 17 years experience anxiety or depression (VanOrman, 2022). With each year, these numbers rise, causing greater concern about children's mental well-being.

One of the behavioral factors contributing to the rising rates of anxiety and depression among young children and teens is excessive technology usage. Numerous studies have linked too much screen time with symptoms of anxiety and depression. These symptoms are caused by overstimulation (as mentioned earlier) and other psychological challenges that are a byproduct of too much screen time, like poor social skills and emotional regulation, lack of self-control, and trouble starting and completing tasks. Additionally, excessive technology usage promotes a sedentary lifestyle that is detrimental to the wellness of growing children. Sitting on the couch or lying down is okay, but not for long periods.

Remember that your child's brain and body continue to grow and develop until they reach their mid-20s. They need ongoing physical activity that gets them moving and mentally stimulated to maintain good mental health. Toddlers, on average, need 30 minutes of physical activity per day, while children between the ages of 6 and 17 need at least an hour of physical activity per day (Cheriyedath, 2024).

Telltale signs that your child needs to get up and move their body include

- feeling sluggish

- struggling to concentrate

- binge eating, particularly when bored

- feeling unhappy or hopeless

- loneliness and social isolation

Screens should not be used as a cure for boredom or as a substitute for socializing. If your child appears bored or lonely, find ways to engage them through a sport, a relaxing walk, or a creative activity. In the absence of friends, accompany your child to events or participate in activities with them, and show enthusiasm while doing it. You can also consider enrolling them in group sports, after-school social clubs, volunteer opportunities, and other social activities that are both fun and mentally stimulating.

In some cases, anxiety can be managed by simply limiting screen time and filling your child's day with more productive and stimulating activities. However, there may be cases when cutting back on technology doesn't help to address issues such as hopelessness, trouble sleeping, loss of appetite, feeling inadequate, being easily angered, or physical complaints like migraines or stomach issues. Make daily observations of your child's behaviors and record patterns or sudden changes in a notebook. If you don't see improvement after several weeks, visit a child psychologist or psychiatrist who can complete a formal assessment of your child's mental health.

Lastly, it's important to add that screens are not a reliable form of therapy. When your child is feeling strong emotions like sadness, anger, loneliness, or overwhelm, encourage them to put away their devices and engage in mindful activities like journaling, deep breathing, or walking to process their emotions. You can also help them create a self-soothing checklist that they can go through whenever they are not feeling well. The checklist should include suggestions of various ways they can calm down and regain a sense of control. Here is an example:

Self-soothing techniques	Check (X)
Take slow and deep breaths, inhaling and exhaling for four counts.	
Close your eyes and count up to 10 slowly, then count down back to 1.	
Stand up and do some basic stretches to release tension in your body.	

Self-soothing techniques	Check (X)
Go outside for a walk or kick a ball.	
Take a relaxing bath or shower to calm your mind.	
Call a friend or family member who knows how to cheer you up.	
Lie down and listen to soothing nature music or instrumentals.	
Review your personal goals and reflect on the progress you have made.	
Write down how you are feeling using "I feel... I need..." statements.	
Write down three things that you are grateful for at this moment.	
Recite three positive affirmations about yourself, like "I am creative."	
Head over to the kitchen and prepare a delicious and healthy snack.	

Self-soothing techniques	Check (X)
Take out your art supplies and draw, paint, or build a DIY craft project.	
Play an offline game like puzzles, outdoor sports, and board games.	
Read something inspirational such as a quote, poem, or book chapter.	

ADHD

A few years ago, Jerrica Sannes, a child expert, caught the attention of the media when she and her husband discovered that her four-year-old son's ADHD-like behaviors were signs of TV addiction (Aubusson, 2021). What seemed to be classic symptoms of ADHD like frequent meltdowns, fidgeting, zoning out, and difficulty managing transitions were a result of watching too many hyperstimulating TV shows nonstop. When Jerrica placed her son on a TV detox and changed his screen habits permanently, his behavior transformed and the symptoms went away.

Another mom, Cynthia McNulty, realized that her nine-year-old son, Matthew, had a video game addiction that was making his ADHD symptoms worse (McNulty, 2022). He suffered from chronic sleep deprivation, emotional outbursts, and mood swings, which made him feel miserable and treat those around him poorly. Whenever Cynthia would restrict him from playing video games, Matthew would experience withdrawal symptoms, similar to an addict. After attending a talk about the dangers of electronics, she set stricter boundaries, limiting video games to weekends only except when the privilege had been earned during weekdays, where he could earn a maximum of an hour a day after school. Despite these boundaries, Matthew still had access to other electronic devices before, during, and after school, as well as during his free time. Recognizing that her boundaries were not enough to address his screen addiction and that she needed more support to tackle this issue, Cynthia consulted a cognitive behavioral therapist.

The therapist asked a profound question that changed Cynthia's perspective on her child's screen habits. She said, "If he were addicted to drugs or alcohol, would you still let him have just a little bit?". It became clear to Cynthia that cutting off electronic devices completely—at least for the short term—was the best decision to restore Matthew's well-being and manage his ADHD symptoms.

True to the addiction rehabilitation process, the first few days were torturous for the family, as Matthew went through withdrawals. He cried, pleaded, fought, and screamed to regain access to his devices, but Cynthia wasn't swayed. Going cold turkey ended up being the best thing for her relationship with her son. Now that the distraction of electronics was out of the way, they could bond. It became a new norm for them to prepare dinners together, play board games, complete crossword puzzles, and do other fun family activities.

Whenever he complained of boredom, Cynthia referred him to a list of offline activities he could do. After three weeks, the rest of the family started noticing positive changes in his attitude and behaviors, citing that he seemed happier and friendlier. The best part is that Matthew noticed these changes too, admitting that he feels better about himself and doesn't miss his video games. Chronic technology usage can be detrimental to developing brains, especially during the first 10 years of children's lives. Research conducted at the University of Alberta found that parents of five-year-olds were five times more likely to misdiagnose their children as having ADHD when they were exposed to two or more hours a day of screen time (Rosenblatt, 2019). This is because screens can interfere with cognitive development, causing symptoms of inattentiveness, hyperactivity, emotional dysregulation, and poor social and communication skills.

On the other hand, children who are diagnosed with ADHD may have more difficulty regulating their screen habits, leading to technology addiction. It is a known fact that children with ADHD struggle to sustain motivation while performing tasks when there isn't an incentive (something exciting and stimulating to trigger a release of dopamine). This is because ADHD causes dopamine deficiencies due to the brain not producing enough dopamine receptors (Littman, 2024). Children with ADHD get bored or unmotivated far more easily than children without the condition because their brains have less dopamine to work with. To reach the same level of motivation as other children, they require stronger incentives, usually in the form of energizing, exciting, and passion-driven tasks.

For instance, if your child has ADHD, they may show a preference for tasks that align with their hobbies and interests and generally avoid or procrastinate on tasks they consider dull or complicated (i.e., tasks that don't feel pleasurable). Technology provides an enormous amount of stimulation for children with ADHD, which makes it difficult for them to resist.

Without setting proper technology boundaries for your child, they can easily become dependent on their electronic devices, becoming hostile or unmotivated when those devices are taken away or when they are instructed to complete other less-interesting offline tasks. Setting stricter screen limits and rules can help your child develop a healthier relationship with technology.

Going cold turkey may not be a strategy necessary for every child; however, the more severe the addiction to technology, the tighter the limits and rules should be. Generally, scheduling screen time into your child's routine and encouraging offline activities may help to reduce ADHD symptoms. It may also be useful to seek a formal diagnosis and get your child started on a treatment plan to address ADHD symptoms in the long term.

ODD

A 2022 study by the University of California San Francisco found a link between too much screen time and disruptive behavior disorders (Nagata et al., 2022). However, various forms of media impact children in different ways. For example, the study showed that chronic social media usage could lead to conduct disorder, a condition that causes one to bully, harass, vandalize, or steal from others. Alternatively, other forms of media like video games, television, video chat, and texting were linked to the development of oppositional defiant disorder (ODD), another type of behavioral condition characterized by argumentative, angry, and vindictive behavior.

Jason Nagata, the lead researcher in the study, highlighted the fact that children can be exposed to violent and inappropriate content online—even when they are not actively searching for it—through links shared by friends, online ads, or content recommended by social media algorithms (Berthold, 2022). Another indirect cause of ODD is sleep deprivation and the lack of physical activity, which impacts children's moods and energies, making them grumpy and unpleasant.

Post-screen time anger and meltdowns are common among children who have become dependent on their electronic devices. Some children may get violent, hurl insults, throw their toys, or become depressed when they are restricted from screens.

The same type of aggressive behavior manifests when they are overstimulated by their screens or when experiencing addiction withdrawals. Behavior disorders like conduct disorder and ODD require medical intervention to address. Several types of psychotherapy like behavior management training, social skills training, cognitive behavior therapy, and family support services are useful in helping your child modify their behaviors. Your child may also need to take medication along with attending therapy sessions if they are diagnosed with a co-occurring disorder like ADHD or depression.

Besides seeking professional help, there are strategies that you can implement at home to reduce disruptive behaviors. For example, before instructing your child to shift from an online activity to an offline activity (e.g., turning the TV off so they can complete their homework), give them enough time to prepare for the transition mentally. Let them know 15 minutes before the expected end time, and again every 5 minutes to follow up and remind them of what is going to happen.

Another suggestion is to reward positive behaviors post-screen time by giving your child access to certain privileges. For example, on days when your child can turn off the TV without putting up a fight, you can reward them with 10 minutes of extra screen time the following day.

If you dislike confrontation and wish to avoid having to approach your child whenever they need to cut off the technology, consider downloading a subscription-based app like Qustudio that automatically sets screen time limits and locks access to the internet, specific apps, or the entire electronic device after a certain number of minutes or hours have passed. Additionally, Qustudio allows you to set technology-free periods during the day so your child can focus on offline tasks like homework, reading, house chores, or physical games. If your child is working on a school project that requires access to the internet, you can block specific apps and websites to encourage them to focus on the task at hand. Other apps similar to Qustudio include Norton Family, FamiSafe, Bark, and Mobicip.

Screen Time Is a Privilege, Not an Entitlement

Children are introduced to screens by their parents. In homes where electronic devices are not easily accessible, children are encouraged to find other ways to curb boredom. As a parent, you control what electronic devices your child can access at home and how often they use them. Remind yourself that screens are not compulsory for your children. At times, they may need to use a cell phone for texts and calls or a computer for research and schoolwork, but they aren't entitled to endless amounts of technology.

Since screens do not contribute to your child's well-being, they should fall at the bottom of the list when structuring their daily routine. At the top of the list should be tasks that are necessary for their physical and personal development such as eating nutritious meals, taking naps, getting physical activity, bonding with loved ones, and engaging in creative and mentally stimulating games and activities. Once these tasks have been checked off the list, they can indulge in a few hours of supervised screen time.

It can also be beneficial to explain to your child that access to screens is a privilege, not the norm. In this way, whenever they are rewarded with a few minutes or hours of screen time, they feel a sense of achievement and are less likely to argue when it's time to get off their screens. Moreover, they have something to look forward to at the end of the day, which helps to sustain their motivation when completing undesirable or difficult tasks during the day. To determine whether you are giving your child too much screen time, go through a developmental checklist and assess how well their primary needs are being met.

If you find that all of their primary needs are being met with ease on the current screen schedule, then the amount of screen time may not be a problem (though, perhaps, you need to make adjustments to the type of media content they are viewing). However, if you are struggling to meet one or more primary needs on the current screen schedule, you must follow through by setting limits.

Here are questions to assess whether your child is achieving their developmental needs:

- Does my child get the recommended hours of sleep per day?

- Does my child consume a healthy and balanced diet?

- Does my child spend enough time bonding with family members?

- Does my child meet with friends for playdates?

- Does my child keep up with schoolwork and show interest in learning?

- Does my child get enough practice learning social and communication skills?

- Does my child have hobbies outside of school that they frequently engage in?

- Does my child get opportunities to exercise, go outdoors, and move their body?

You may find it easier to ensure your child achieves these developmental needs when they are younger. Preteens and teenagers have more freedom to choose what activities they want to engage in.

Some, depending on their personalities, may not show interest in school, physical exercise, spending quality time with family, or maintaining friendships. Be considerate of their needs and wishes while also being firm about your family's nonnegotiables.

For example, your child may procrastinate while completing homework, but during homework hours, they are strictly not allowed to access their electronic devices unless it is required for their schoolwork. Or maybe your child doesn't enjoy socializing but, to maintain social connections, you might require them to pick up a sport, join a social club, or volunteer at a local shelter. Find ways to compromise with your child so that they can express who they are while achieving a balanced lifestyle.

Most importantly, do not allow your child to use technology as a substitute for their developmental needs. Screens should not replace family bonding time, in-person social interactions, physical activity, or quality sleep. Instead, screens should be a reward earned after a productive day spent on tasks vital to their well-being.

Chapter 3:

The Physical Effects of Screen Time

Even the technology that promises to unite us, divides us. Each of us is now electronically connected to the globe, and yet we feel utterly alone. —
Dan Brown

How Screens Impact Your Child's Growing Body

So far, we have looked at several ways where excessive screen time impacts your child's cognitive well-being, such as by causing brain development and mental health issues.

In this chapter, we examine the impact of technology on your child's physical well-being, identifying some of the challenges they might experience if the proper screen limits and boundaries are not set.

Physical activity stimulates bone and muscle growth, protects your immune system, and ensures that your metabolism is functioning properly. Moreover, body movement has a positive effect on the mind and operates as a natural stress reliever and sedative.

Studies have shown that young children and teenagers who live active lifestyles by playing sports or working out are more emotionally resilient than children who don't (Li et al., 2022). Physical activity can also help young children learn gross motor skills such as how to use their large muscles to jump, walk, balance, climb, or catch and throw objects.

Whenever your child is watching TV, playing a game on their tablet, texting, or scrolling through social media, they are typically sitting or lying down. For those few hours, no movement takes place. In cases of technology addiction, where different screens consume most of your child's time, they might get little to no movement each day, which can lead to poor physical health and risk of chronic diseases like diabetes, asthma, obesity, visual impairments, and hearing impairments.

This doesn't mean that your child should be up and running the whole day or that sitting down to watch a show or play a video game is bad. Striking a good balance between active and sedentary activities is key. There are times during the day when your child will need to sit or lie down, but this should be balanced with activities that allow them to move their body.

If your child cannot go outside due to the weather or other factors, encourage physical movements like stretching, scavenger hunts, aerobic exercises, dancing, or doing chores inside the house. When sitting down, encourage your child to use the correct posture, maintain a healthy distance from screens to protect their eyes, and take frequent movement breaks to stretch their legs or drink water.

Below is a breakdown of the physical risks posed by excessive screen time and what you can do to manage them and improve your child's physical well-being.

Sleep Disruptions

We can agree that sleep is an important aspect of our children's day. They need to get those hours of rest to replenish their energy from a day's worth of talking, running, thinking, and playing. Older children need sleep to process a large sum of information while studying, reading, watching shows, socializing with their peers, or solving complex personal or academic problems.

Getting quality sleep each night is like hitting the "reset" button and getting the mind and body back to factory settings in preparation for the next day. When your child doesn't get sufficient sleep, they may end up developing both physical and mental health issues, since their bodies aren't able to recharge. Many factors might interfere with your child's quality of sleep, but the one that we will focus on is the chronic use of technology.

Excessive screen time causes sleep delays and disruptions due to several reasons. The first is that electronic devices often emit a blue light that can be brightened or dimmed (on some devices). This blue light confuses the brain, making it appear to be daytime. As a result, the hormone known as melatonin that naturally helps your child fall asleep is blocked and they may find themselves staying awake throughout the night.

Giving your child melatonin supplements can assist with inducing sleep. However, they may seem ineffective when your child is chronically dependent on their electronic devices. Technology can also make it difficult to establish a structured sleep and wake time for your child.

There is always "just one more" game or episode that they need to watch before winding down and preparing for bed. This phenomenon is known as "revenge bedtime procrastination," and is likely to occur whenever children don't feel like they didn't have sufficient leisure time during the day. Nighttime is the only chance they get during the day for free time, so they might binge on technology and delay going to sleep. Coupled with this, media content can mentally and physically stimulate your child, leading to bouts of energy, mood swings, or anxious thoughts.

Stimulation is appropriate in the mornings and afternoons, but never in the evenings when your child needs to gradually settle down and calm their mind. Watching hyperstimulating shows keeps your child's mind working and sometimes triggers stress and anxiety. Processing these emotions and thoughts and returning to a peaceful state can take several hours, reducing the total hours your child spends sleeping.

Staying on the subject of mental health, poor sleep has been linked with conditions like anxiety and depression, which creates a perpetual cycle of sleep deprivation (Chen, 2023). This also works in reverse: Children who are exhibiting signs of anxiety and depression may struggle to shut down at night and go to sleep. In severe cases, they may develop a type of sleep disorder known as insomnia, which makes it difficult for them to fall or asleep or stay asleep for a full night.

Does the Type of Electronic Device Make a Difference?

You may be wondering whether some screens are better than others when it comes to impacting your child's sleep. There haven't been many studies comparing the types of devices and their effects on sleep; however, we know that being exposed to any type of screen an hour before bedtime can cause sleep delays or disruptions (Pacheco & Vyas, 2023).

With that said, some experts suggest that screens that are held close to the face such as smartphones or tablets increase the exposure to blue light and negatively affect the body's sleep-wake cycle. Furthermore, viewing screens in a dark room enhances the blue light emitted from the device and impacts melatonin levels too.

Professor of Pediatrics, Maida Chen, highlighted in an article that the type of content viewed can also affect sleep quality. She identified fast-paced content found on social media apps and gaming platforms to be the most harmful because of how they stimulate the brain (Chen, 2023).

Additionally, she found that fast-paced content can reduce the amount of time your child spends in deep non-dream sleep—the stage of sleep that is necessary for mental and physical restoration.

Since the brain needs several hours to process the fast-paced content viewed, it cannot fully relax and achieve a state of calm, even when your child asleep. If your child has viewed disturbing or triggering content before bed, they may struggle to fall asleep or have nightmares and uncomfortable sleep when they do. This explains why their sleep might be interrupted during the night or why they might wake up with body aches and feel unrested.

In the long run, sleep deprivation not only affects your child's physical and mental health, but their emotional well-being and performance too. They may struggle to concentrate at school, maintain a healthy body weight, maintain a positive attitude, or build meaningful relationships with their peers due to the lack of focus and self-regulation. Some children may develop behavior problems such as anger issues, impulsivity, social anxiety, or addictions to food and other substances as a way to cope with chronic sleep deprivation and the psychological impact it has on their lives.

How to Create a Healthy, Screen-Free Bedtime Routine

To address the negative effects of screen time on your child's sleep, the best solution is to reduce or completely eliminate screens before bedtime, if possible. There is no value that screens offer your child during that time of day because their mind and body is preparing to unwind and eventually go to sleep. Stimulating activities will only delay the sleep cycle and reduce the total hours they spend asleep.

Establishing a screen-free bedtime routine requires implementing several strategies at home. Note that these strategies need not only apply to your child but can apply to the whole family to improve everyone's quality of sleep. Consider the tips below to improve your child's bedtime routine.

Set a Bedtime Curfew

Be clear and consistent on the time your child goes to bed. The curfew can change for weekdays and weekends, but only by a few hours to ensure your child is able to adjust to the different times with ease.

The benefit of setting a bedtime curfew is that you can work backward and assess what time electronic devices need to be taken away (at least an hour before bed), what time your child needs to eat their last meal for the day, what time house chores need to be complete, and so on.

Older children may want to have a say on when their curfew should be, so be open to having the discussion with them and reaching a healthy compromise. Once the curfew has been set, however, it cannot be negotiated or changed without valid reasons.

Discover Relaxing Bedtime Habits

Your child doesn't need to be bored when their devices are taken away. During those few hours before bed, you can encourage them to practice habits that are calming to the mind and body. Not only will your child stay preoccupied, but they will also mentally and physically prepare themselves for going to sleep. Different bedtime habits will appeal to children at different ages. For example, a toddler might enjoy listening to soothing background music or playing with toys in a warm bath. An older child might prefer to play an active sport or game that burns surplus energy, making them feel tired. Teenagers may have a lot on their mind and benefit from journaling, creating to-do lists, calling a friend, or having motivational conversations with Mom and Dad. All of these tasks calm children's nervous systems and help to induce sleep.

Visual Impairments

In the previous section, we spoke about the dangers of blue light emission on sleep. However, the same blue light can put a strain on your child's eyes, especially when they frequently stand near to the TV screen or hold their tablet or smartphone close to their face.

A number of risks are posed to your child's vision when they are constantly exposed to blue light. We will go over each of them in the sections below.

Eye Fatigue

Eye fatigue, formally known as asthenopia, is a condition characterized by strained eyes, which can cause headaches, droopy eyes, tiredness, and dimness of vision. It typically affects children who spend a large portion of their day glued to their screens, whether for educational purposes (such as online homeschooling) or entertainment. Eye fatigue can make it difficult for them to maintain focus on an object, read text (especially when it's written in small font), or keep their eyes open.

Dry Eyes

Dry eyes are a symptoms of eye fatigue and normally occur when children have been watching screens for an extended period with few breaks in between. It can also be caused by not enough blinking while focusing on screens, which subsequently dries out their eyes. This condition can lead to redness of the eyes due to the dryness or constant rubbing.

Nearsightedness

Children who frequently sit close to TV screens or place their handheld devices close to their faces may suffer from nearsightedness, formally known as myopia: a vision condition that makes objects nearby look clear but those farther away appear blurry. Research studies have found that spending too much time indoors is linked to the development of myopia and that children who are exposed to natural sunlight can reduce this risk and lead to healthy vision (Malik, 2021).

How to Protect Your Child's Eye Health From Exposure to Screens

Your child is exposed to screens at home and school, so completely removing them may not be the feasible solution for ensuring good eye health. Instead, you can consider different strategies to minimize the strong effect that screen lighting has on your child's eyes.

Below are some tips to get you started.

Adjust the Screen Size and Distance

A great place to start is to reposition your TV screens at home to ensure they are placed at a healthy distance from your child. Lower them slightly from adult level to avoid your child having to strain their neck and eyes looking up at them. Additionally, place them 10 feet away from couches or sitting areas to create enough distance.

If your child is holding a smartphone or tablet, teach them to hold it a foot away from their face. When using laptops and computers, they should sit at least two feet away for comfortable viewing. Another useful tip is to swap small screens with large screens to avoid squinting and straining your child's eyes.

Implement the 20–20–20–2 Rule

To get your child and the rest of the family familiar with maintaining a healthy distance from their screens, introduce them to the 20–20–20 rule. The instructions are simple: Focus on something for 20 seconds, blinking 20 times, and standing 20 feet away (Malik, 2021). The additional "2" stands for 2 hours of outdoor play each day to balance screen time with fun physical activity. To make this rule interesting, consider gamifying it and offering tokens and rewards each time your child or other family members follow it.

Schedule Regular Eye Screenings

Don't wait until your child complains about their eyes to schedule a routine eye exam. At minimum, children should visit an optometrist for a vision screening once a year, beginning at birth. However, if they do experience occasional dry eyes, red eyes, blurry vision, or eye discomfort, schedule an appointment as soon as you can. If serious vision problems are found, the doctor may refer your child to a pediatric ophthalmologist.

Purchase a Pair of Blue-Light Filtering Glasses

If your child attends online homeschooling and spends much of their days watching screens, consider purchasing blue-light filtering glasses that they can wear during school hours when they are online. As the name suggests, these glasses reduce the amount of blue light your child absorbs from their screens, thereby protecting their eye sight. To reduce the emission of blue light, you can also adjust the brightness of your child's smartphone, tablet, or laptop's screens, opting for a warmer yellow or orange light that is comfortable for their eyes.

Body Aches and Pain

One of the main reasons screen time is seen as an unproductive use of time is that you are forced to sit or lie down for an extended period. It may be relaxing for the first 10–15 minutes, but as time goes on, your body may start experiencing discomfort. Body aches and pains are common among children who spend too much time on screens. The discomfort is caused by poor posture and uncomfortable sitting positions. Moreover, maintaining one position for a long time can cause muscle spasms and tension.

Two issues that children complain about are their back and neck. Upper back pain is caused by slouching shoulders while using devices like computers or smartphones, while lower back pain occurs when sitting at a desk for several hours without getting the necessary lower back support. Hunching over screens, like when texting or watching a show, can place significant strain on their neck muscles and spinal discs, causing pain and discomfort. Another problem that contributes to this is constantly looking up or down at screens and maintaining unnatural neck and back positions for a long time. To fix these issues, good posture is recommended. Simple practices like relaxing the shoulders, sitting upright (with the correct back support), viewing screens at eye level, and using cushions to sit comfortably on chairs can support the spine.

If your child completes their homework or eats meals at a desk or table, check that the height of the chair is proportionate to the height of the desk or table and that their feet are rested on the floor (consider buying a footstep if your child's feet don't reach the floor). Their arms should be able to rest on the table without having to move their shoulders, and the computer keyboard and mouse need to also be within arms' reach without having to lift their back off the chair, bend over, or engage other muscles.

Lastly, taking movement breaks is crucial to maintaining good posture and relieving muscle tension. Movement breaks can be short five-minute rest breaks that allow your child to get up and stretch their legs or move around. These breaks promote healthy blood circulation and can reduce muscle stiffness. Mentally, they give your child an opportunity to get some fresh air, shift their focus to another task, or attend to emergency needs like using the restroom or drinking water.

Weight Management

Excessive screen viewing creates what we defined in the introduction of the book as a "zombie effect": a passive trance-like state where your child is focused solely on what they are watching. When food and beverages are consumed in this state, it is possible for your child to overeat due to being unaware of the quantity of food they are eating or when they feel full.

Research has found an association between snacking or consuming meals and TV viewing. One study went a step further and discovered that children who had TV screens in their bedrooms were more likely to gain excessive weight than children who didn't (Harguth, 2021). Another association between junk food marketing in online ads and obesity was also found, proving that the more food content children are exposed to online, the more intense their food cravings become.

The lack of physical activity creates weight challenges for children who haven't found a balance between online and offline experiences. Even though it's possible to stay active and move around indoors, the best form of exercise happens in the playground, sports ground, or backyard. Many children are lucky enough to get their recommended hour of physical activity while at school. However, for those who are homeschooled or attend online school, making an effort to leave the house for an hour can support healthy weight management.

Something else to consider are the types of snacks that are kept in the house. There is a big difference between snacking on fruits and snacking on ice cream or candy. Both snacks are sweet, but the former is packed with nutritional value and fewer calories, making it the healthier option. Look inside your pantry and assess what type of snacks you have to offer your child. It's okay to have some unhealthy options but these shouldn't be easily accessible to your child. Normal TV snacks should consist of healthy options like fruits, chopped vegetables, nuts and dried fruit, crackers, oatmeal cookies, and fruity popsicles.

Adopting healthy rituals such as eating screen-free meals together or going on afternoon walks can keep the whole family active and allow you to manage your weight. You can also challenge yourselves in group sports or by eating healthy meals during the week and deciding on a delectable treat that you can reward yourselves with on the weekends. Make the rituals fun and get everyone involved to emphasize the importance of fitness and healthy habits.

Ultimately, maintaining a healthy lifestyle is achievable, even with screen exposure. The trick is to help your child find ways of enjoying their screen time without compromising their sleep or body. Being fit, alert, and strong should ideally climb to the top of their to-do list, while catching up on TV shows or video games should fall to the bottom.

Part 2:

The Psychological Implications

of Excessive Technology

Usage

Chapter 4:

The Impact of Technology on Self-Concept and Self-Esteem

People who smile while they are alone used to be called insane, until we invented smartphones and social media. —Mokokoma Mokhonoana

Self-Concept Formation

In the book's first part, we explored the myriad of ways in which screen time affects cognitive and physical development. A key message that was emphasized throughout was the importance of helping your child strike a balance between online and offline activities to ensure they are addressing their developmental needs and reducing the risk of chronic mental and physical conditions. In this second part of the book, we will examine the psychological implications of screen time, focusing primarily on how the overconsumption of technology impacts how children perceive themselves and others. To do this, we need first to define what self-concept means and how it relates to your child. Self-concept is a psychological term that refers to the ideas you possess about who you are. These ideas can be empowering or disempowering, depending on the collection of thoughts and beliefs you hold about yourself. Self-concept is also informed by how you see yourself in connection to other people. Seeing yourself as being better than others or less than others impacts your attitudes and behaviors in online and physical settings.

Shifting the focus to your child, having a strong and stable self-concept gives your child the confidence to step into rooms or join conversations and feel inspired to express who they are. Their self-beliefs are reassuring and aligned with their values, making it easier for them to speak with conviction, disagree respectfully, and stand out from the crowd. A weak and unstable self-concept has the opposite effect. Your child may avoid social settings where they will be expected to share their thoughts and ideas due to being self-conscious, afraid of criticism or rejection, or underestimating the value they can provide to the group.

To avoid human interactions, they might opt for online interactions with social media users or fellow gamers where the engagement is less direct and the conversations don't require vulnerability. Online interactions can provide a sense of belonging, to some extent, especially in tight-knit subculture communities. However, when your child relies too heavily on online interactions, they miss out on the opportunity to practice social and communication skills and develop social awareness.

Social awareness is a skill that cannot be taught through technology. It requires experience navigating different social situations, engaging with people from different social and cultural backgrounds, and having the psychological tools to solve social problems such as knowing how to negotiate, resolve conflict, and set healthy boundaries. When your child doesn't have social awareness, they may feel caught off guard whenever they come across specific personalities or situations that require specific skill sets.

Real-life social exchanges require a unique set of skills that can only be developed through making physical contact with people. The inability to pick up on social cues, read body language, and understand social etiquette and norms can make your child the target of bullying or social alienation since they are often misunderstood.

Part of what makes us feel happy about ourselves is knowing that we are accepted and validated by our peers. When your child doesn't receive the social acceptance and validation they need to feel whole and fulfilled, they can start to question their identity and self-worth.

Therefore, to build a healthy and stable self-concept, it's crucial to expose your child to offline social activities from an early age—as young as three years old. This could be as simple as attending play dates. The goal is to get them feeling comfortable around strangers, specifically their peers, and willing to share toys, initiate play, spark conversations, and demonstrate empathy. The positive feedback your child receives from other children and adults validates their self-concept and allows them to explore their identity in a stress-free and nurturing environment.

As they get older, your child will start to reflect on their identity about other people, discovering what makes them unique, what makes them likable to others, what social behaviors are acceptable and unacceptable, and what behaviors help them build strong relationships. These insights are what make your child feel confident and competent in who they are.

The Good and Bad Side of Digital Identities

A relatively new concept that is tied to self-concept is digital identity, which describes how we represent ourselves online. We all have digital identities, even those of us who may not be active regularly online. Our digital identities are shaped by the type of content we relate to and endorse, the comments and feedback we offer, and the people or communities we engage with. Other aspects of our digital identities are the images, videos, social media posts, articles, email addresses, and other personal details we share. This information says a lot about who we are, what we are passionate about, and how we would like to be perceived by others.

Having digital identities is not a bad thing. Besides allowing us to make financial transactions, purchase goods, build our brands, and find relatable content, they can also help us connect with like-minded people and form supportive online communities. The danger is not so much that we have these digital personas, but that sometimes, particularly with young people, these personas can distort our perception of reality.

The excessive use of social media or the internet contributes to a growing number of children who battle with low self-esteem, anxiety, and depression. One of the reasons for this has to do with how children represent themselves online versus how their lifestyles are designed in real life. Online platforms and communities tend to level the playing field and enable anyone, regardless of their age, gender, income, status, or education to become highly influential and gain a large following. Furthermore, the standards set online are typically different than the standards set in real life.

For example, a young teenage girl can trend online and get 1,000 "likes" for writing an engaging post or uploading a beautiful photo. This may be followed by 500 social media users telling her how awesome she is. In real life, this kind of social validation would be given to celebrities with thousands of fans, not a young girl who is still in school and may only know 50 people in total. The contrast between her digital identity and real-life circumstances can make it difficult for her to determine which aspects of her personality or real or not. Moreover, she may feel disconnected from her real-life support system, who don't perceive her in the same way her online followers do.

Another example of the difference between online and real-life standards has to do with lifestyle choices. Since online platforms and communities can be customized to provide niche content and information, children can be exposed to a wide range of lifestyles that they may not have access to in real life. Engaging with those posts, images, and videos can create confusion about what a normal lifestyle should consist of. For example, a young teenage boy who follows successful investors and entrepreneurs online may develop an unrealistic understanding of wealth building. Based on the content he watches, he might assume that anybody can become rich and that it doesn't have to take several years to accumulate wealth. Additionally, he may associate success with materialistic gains, believing that to truly become successful, he needs to possess certain luxuries.

It can be difficult to convince a child to not believe or endorse everything that they see online. The unpleasant truth is that the majority of the content posted online has been edited and manipulated to reinforce harmful ideas, beliefs, and expectations. Brands and businesses make billions in profit from the insecurities of naive young people who would be willing to purchase products or make changes to their lifestyles so that they can fit in and gain social acceptance. Apart from brands and businesses, another aspect of the problem is the significant pressure young people experience from their peers to conform. Think of how quickly dance challenges go viral on TikTok or sensational news spreads on X. The fear that many young children have is that by not conforming, they can be alienated from their peer group and seen as unprogressive. This is especially true in cases where children rely heavily on their online presence and connections for validation. In contrast, those who have managed to build friendships offline may not be so easily pressured to conform. They are not extremely sensitive to online criticism and judgment because they have built a stable identity and community of supporters in real life.

The same goes with making comparisons. Children who don't have a strong friendship base offline tend to compete and compare their lives to online users. However, those who do, know that people's backgrounds and lifestyles are nuanced and that not everybody lives or aspires to obtain the same goals.

Cyberbullying

One of the challenges of social media is the way it desensitizes people to what would be considered social taboos or inappropriate behaviors. It is common to scroll past images of half-naked women, videos of vandalism and physical assault, or read insults and offensive comments that social media users wouldn't have the courage to repeat in real life. Rarely do people pause and consider how their words and actions would make others feel before posting.

As a result of desensitization, cyberbullying and online criticism have become common among children and adults. We can define cyberbullying as the deliberate act of intimidating, harassing, threatening, or humiliating someone online through various forms of manipulation and passive aggression. What makes cyberbullying different from traditional bullying is that the perpetrator and victim don't have to physically confront each other. Harmful messages are shared through electronic devices and can sometimes be indirect, such as spreading a rumor or exposing personal information about someone without tagging them or mentioning their name.

A 2022 study from the Pew Research Center found that 46% of teenagers between the ages of 13 and 17 report having experienced at least one of the following cyberbullying behaviors in their lifetime (Vogels, 2022):

- physical threats

- name-calling

- false rumors being spread about them

- being sent images they didn't ask for

- having explicit images of them shared without giving consent

- frequently being asked where they are, who they are with, or what they are doing by someone other than their parents

The actual number of teens who are victims of cyberbullying may be more than what the statistics show because many cases of cyberbullying don't get reported. Due to the desensitized nature of social media, many abusive behaviors go unnoticed and unpunished, which makes victims less motivated to speak up and report the perpetrator. Moreover, there still exists a stigma around bullying where victims are seen as weak and vulnerable while perpetrators are seen as powerful and undefeatable. Therefore, children who are victims of this unacceptable behavior might end up being silenced.

Cyberbullying is a form of emotional abuse and should be seen as such. The bully may be younger or older than your child, but their words are lethal weapons that can trigger emotional wounds, self-esteem issues, body image issues, and past trauma. It's also not easy to just forget about cyberbullying incidents, particularly when they are orchestrated by a group rather than an individual, and attacks are coming from all sides. Through the ordeal, your child's sense of dignity, respect, and self-worth are put on the line, and it can take years to process the hurt.

Signs that your child could be a victim of cyberbullying include

- a shift of mood before and after going on social media

- spending more time alone in their bedroom

- loss of interest in the hobbies they used to enjoy

- being secretive about their phone or computer activities

- spending less time with friends and family

- unexplained physical symptoms like migraines, panic attacks, or stomach problems

- avoiding certain public spaces, gatherings, or groups of people

- making passing statements about self-harming or performing self-destructive behaviors

There are many ways that you can support your child from cyberbullies. The first thing to do is to ensure that your child is safe. Encourage them to set their accounts to private and avoid accepting requests or following people they don't know. They should also regularly update their passwords and immediately delete their profile if it has been hacked. Using the "mute," "unfollow," or "block" features can also help your child disengage with bullies and potential stalkers. Going back and forth with cyberbullies is never a good strategy. Not only does the attention satisfy them, it can escalate the situation and lead to worse outcomes. Encourage your child to stop all forms of communication with cyberbullies and refrain from commenting on posts that are triggering. In cases where your child's name is mentioned or there is sufficient evidence via direct messages or posts to prove they are being harassed, threatened, or blackmailed, gather the information and approach law enforcement officials who can assist with further investigations. Counseling is another avenue to explore when seeking to offer your child more professional support and tools on how to approach cyberbullies in the future.

On the odd occasion, you may discover that your child is the perpetrator of cyberbullying, meaning they are the one harassing, insulting, intimidating, or spreading rumors and sensitive information about other people. Children often bully when they are angry, sad, or unfulfilled but don't have the proper coping skills to process their thoughts and emotions. They might also bully when they are insecure about an aspect of their identity or life situation. To cover their deep inferiority complex, they become overly critical and judgmental of others, which gives them a false sense of superiority.

Another reason why they might bully is if they are a victim of bullying at home. Reflect on the relationships your child has with you, your spouse or partner, or their siblings. Is it possible that they are being mistreated, teased, called names, or criticized? Do they feel safe expressing who they are? How much emotional support do they get from home? This may also be a great time to reflect on your parenting approach and whether it is suitable for your child. Each child is unique and may require different strategies to get through to them. Study your child's personality and what they respond favorably to and adjust your behaviors to strengthen your parent–child bond and make it safe for them to open up and share their feelings.

Sometimes, what may be perceived as bullying could be a lack of social skills and emotional intelligence. For instance, your child may not be aware that certain topics aren't discussed online or that sharing someone's sensitive information is a breach of trust and can hurt them. In addition to this, your child may lack personal boundaries, making it difficult for them to assess limits to what they can say or post about. Thus, your child's intentions may not be to bully others, but, due to their low social awareness, they find themselves in trouble. Social skills training and cognitive behavioral therapy (CBT) can help your child learn appropriate social conduct so they can modify their behaviors in different settings. It's also important to emphasize to your child that bullying of any kind is unacceptable and that there are no excuses for treating others poorly.

Strategies for Building a Positive Self-Image in a Digital World

Your child needs to know they don't have to impress others or seek validation online. Being authentically themselves is enough, and the right people will be naturally drawn to them. To enjoy the experience of being part of online communities, they need to have the confidence to align their real-life identity with their digital identity. This can be achieved through building a positive self-image. Here are some strategies you can introduce to your child and practice together.

Invest in Your Life Offline

Having a vibrant and satisfying life outside of social media and the internet gives your child a haven to run to whenever they need a break from their screens. If they are extraverted, encourage them to find and join groups of like-minded people who meet up often to socialize and exchange ideas or perform activities. If they are introverted, help them discover their hobbies and invest time in mastering them. Additionally, help your child come up with a list of offline activities they can practice to cope with stress, anxiety, boredom, or loneliness in order to distract themselves from social media. For instance, they might enjoy painting, going to therapy, volunteering, exercising, or playing with their pets. Teach them that social media isn't a place to "dump emotions" but rather to listen, learn, share, and validate others.

Improve Your Self-Talk

When browsing through the internet, your child will come across people who are doing better than them and some who are worse off than them. They may be tempted to compete and compare themselves to those who they consider superior and successful. However, this only leads to greater feelings of insecurity and feeling unsatisfied with their life and progress.

The dialogue that your child has with themselves, known as self-talk, determines the pleasant and unpleasant thoughts and emotions they feel about themselves or about other people. Negative self-talk, which is characterized by offensive language and criticism, makes your child feel smaller and less competent than other people. To help your child improve their self-talk, promote the habit of speaking kind, honest, and empowering words at home, whether they are referring to themselves or their family members. Positive self-talk can be as simple as swapping "can't" with "capable" and focusing on strengths and opportunities instead of weaknesses and limitations.

Focus on Your Message, Not Others' Opinions

Before posting anything, it's always good to pause and reflect on how your image, video, or post could be interpreted. However, being overly concerned about how the message will be received can compromise authenticity. Individuality is not celebrated enough online due to users being afraid of potential backlash. But without expressing unique views, social media becomes a game of following trends rather than setting trends. Teach your child to be intentional about the thoughts and ideas they share, focusing on why they are sharing them (i.e., the deeper purpose behind their posts), and not on what other people will think. When social media is used intentionally, it can be a space for sharing knowledge, advocating for worthy causes, spreading positivity, and being a positive role model to other users.

Your child needs to build an identity that doesn't revolve around what people think or feel about them. The internet is not a place to build personalities. It's a place to express who you already are. Regularly praise and compliment your child for qualities and behaviors they display that make them special. When they are continuously validated at home and by their circle of friends, they won't chase after validation online.

Chapter 5:

Interpersonal Behaviors and Attitudes

Smartwatches don't keep you fit, activity does. Do you really need to know what your pulse rate is, every minute? —Abhijit Naskar

The Necessity of Social Skills Development

In the previous chapter, we discussed the impact of excessive screen time on building a healthy and stable self-concept. Many young people can get carried away by their digital identities, overlooking the need for face-to-face social interactions and relationships. As a result, they miss out on the opportunity to build and practice social skills, which are fundamental for establishing strong bonds with others. Children start developing social skills before they can even talk. By making social observations, recognizing facial expressions and their meaning, and reacting appropriately to social cues, they learn how to engage with other people effectively. Due to developmental delays, learning disabilities, or attachment issues, some children show a lack of desire to engage with others. They may avoid eye contact, prefer playing alone, refuse to share, throw tantrums when they are placed outside of their comfort zones, or show a preference for only a few adults whom they trust.

As we have already explored in Part 1, early exposure to technology can also contribute to poor social skills. Screens don't require young children to talk or engage with other people. Furthermore, depending on the quality of the shows or games, they may not be exposed to educational content that might improve their speaking abilities. Technology can also be socially isolating, keeping your child indoors and away from their peers. As such, they may develop social anxiety and avoid group play, group sports, or social gatherings.

What's more, when children are not used to sharing, negotiating, initiating conversations, resolving conflict, and taking on different perspectives, they may develop antisocial behaviors such as hitting or biting others, yelling or making demands, not responding to instructions, being bossy or a bully, or emotionally shutting down. They may have learned these behaviors from the programs they watch on-screen, the videos they have been exposed to, or picking up unhealthy habits of family members like older siblings. These antisocial behaviors become normalized coping mechanisms for when they are feeling stressed or overwhelmed.

It's important to understand the role and impact of parental involvement in teaching social skills to children. The behaviors that children adopt and learn when they are young are, to some extent, based on behaviors modeled by their parents, or, at the very least, permitted by their parents. Young children don't know the difference between appropriate and inappropriate behaviors; they have to be taught and encouraged to practice what's socially acceptable. When parents lack social skills such as empathy, emotional regulation, perspective-taking, emotional intelligence, and positive conflict resolution, they set a bad example for their children. For instance, when a parent resolves a conflict by raising their voice, name-calling, or adopting the silent treatment, their child learns to do the same whenever they are faced with conflict.

Instead of performing healthy social behaviors like taking time out or sharing their feelings when they are overwhelmed, the child might seek attention by yelling, saying hurtful words, using the silent treatment, and so on. Modeling proper social skills can have the opposite effect, encouraging the child to learn positive ways to express themselves. Parents who turn a blind eye to their children's antisocial behaviors teach them that there are no consequences for inappropriate social conduct. This may be acceptable at home, but it certainly isn't tolerated at schools, in shopping malls, in other people's homes, and later, in the workplace.

Studies have shown that while permissive parents are loving and emotionally attuned to their children's needs, they struggle to enforce discipline and set boundaries, which makes it difficult for children to recognize unacceptable behaviors and work toward rectifying them (Cherry, 2022). These children may grow up with a false sense of entitlement, believing that life is mostly about seeking pleasure and avoiding pain. Due to having few rules and structure as children, they may also experience the following social challenges as they get older:

- low academic achievement, resulting from their parents not establishing reasonable goals and expectations that they can diligently work toward

- making poor decisions and life choices as a result of not being taught right from wrong and given guidelines on how to solve problems effectively

- higher risk of rebellious behavior, getting in trouble with the law, dropping out of school and other delinquent behaviors, as well as substance use problems

- aggressive behaviors and low emotional understanding as a result of not knowing how to process emotions and deal with stressful situations

- low self-regulation and self-control, such as not being able to manage time effectively or address self-destructive habits (e.g., binging on food, watching too much television, or turning to other mind-numbing behaviors).

As you can see, parents have a significant impact on their children's ability to learn and practice good social skills. Modeling positive social behaviors such as active listening, showing empathy, being cooperative, and setting healthy boundaries helps children understand the behavioral standards to strive for. Additionally, adopting a more balanced parenting style where children are emotionally validated but still given structure and guidance on how to conduct themselves (and disciplined when they perform undesirable behavior) allows them to feel confident in exploring the world, following rules, and building healthy relationships with others.

Promoting Positive Social Skills at Home

Not all hope is lost. Regardless of your child's age, you can expose them to social skills and encourage them to keep practicing. The human brain stops growing at the age of 25, but learning doesn't stop at that age, since new skills and behaviors can be learned well into adulthood. This also means that if you need to brush up on your social skills, it's not too late. Take this as a self-improvement opportunity to become a better role model for your child.

When teaching your child social skills, start with the foundational skills that can set them up for success in various areas of their life. We'll cover a few in the sections below.

Survival Social Skills

To stay safe, avoid conflict, and get along with people, your child will need to develop survival skills such as active listening, following instructions, abiding by the rules, and being cooperative. Write down a list of the common social situations that your child encounters regularly and the skills required to achieve positive outcomes. For example, your child may need to make friends, listen to their school teacher, regulate their emotions in the classroom, follow house rules, and know how to adjust when visiting other households. Use role-play to reenact these social situations and practice acceptable behaviors. For instance, when practicing desirable classroom behaviors, you might play the role of a teacher and your child plays the role of the student.

Interpersonal Skills

Another set of skills that your child needs to learn is interpersonal skills. These are skills that help to facilitate strong and positive relationships with others. A big component of interpersonal skills building is increasing your child's self-awareness so that they are aware of their strengths and weaknesses in social situations, as well as how their behaviors come across to others. Your child may have good intentions by acting a certain way; however, if their behavior isn't perceived positively, it can lead to misunderstandings. Types of interpersonal skills to teach your child include open communication, sharing, waiting for their turn, joining an activity, politeness, giving and taking compliments, asking questions, and being curious about others.

Conflict Resolution Skills

Disagreements are inevitable in relationships, and your child needs to be prepared for having a difference of opinion with others, being misunderstood or wrongly accused, being left out by their peers, and having to stand up for themselves. If your child is validated at home, let them know that other people may not be as supportive or accommodating of their needs as their family is. Types of conflict resolution skills to teach your child include disagreeing respectfully, seeking mutually beneficial outcomes, learning to self-reflect and apologize for mistakes, communicating assertively, being willing to compromise, and collaborating with others to achieve shared goals.

Relationship Management

Building and maintaining relationships becomes critical for older children who are in their late teens and preparing to transition into adulthood. The relationships that they form at this stage of their life determine the quality of their support system. Your child needs to learn positive ways to nurture long-term relationships, which might include being helpful and reliable, showing a willingness to learn from others, making an effort to stay connected with their peers, and diversifying their social connections by getting to know people from different backgrounds.

Part of relationship management also involves understanding that people's needs and expectations are not the same and that how you approach one person may not be appropriate when approaching another person. Teach your child how to adjust their attitude, demeanor, and behaviors depending on the people they are surrounded by. For example, your child's speech and body posture must change when they are speaking to a classmate versus a school teacher to show respect and reflect the nature of their relationship (i.e., more formal than casual). Developing these social skills will take time, so be easy on your child as they attempt to catch up and learn what they should've developed when they were younger. If needed, you can take your child to therapy and get expert guidance and tools to hone these skills. You may also benefit from attending therapy sessions so that you can learn positive ways to support your child in the current phase of their life and ensure they are prepared for the future.

Empathy and Emotional Intelligence

Studies have found that too much technology use can lead to emotional deficits, such as poor emotional regulation, a lack of empathy, and low emotional intelligence (Sato, 2024). These issues normally start in childhood but become visible and progressively worse during adolescence. What's interesting is that sometimes, children can be mistakenly diagnosed with ASD when, in fact, their symptoms are caused by chronic screen exposure.

Michael Nagel, who is an Associate Professor at the University of Sunshine Coast, explains the association between excessive screen time and autism symptoms in a book that he coauthored, titled *Becoming Autistic* (Nagel & Sharman, 2023). Citing his work and studies from other researchers, he notes that children who are addicted to technology display poor theory of mind, which is the inability to understand the emotions and thoughts of others. Other classic autism symptoms they may display include the lack or avoidance of eye contact, inattention, and trouble controlling their emotions.

These findings do not suggest that too much screen time can make children autistic; however, they can develop symptoms that look and feel like autism. The good news, however, is that these symptoms can be reversed by undergoing a therapeutic recovery process, which can include treatments like occupational therapy, speech and language training, and cognitive behavioral therapy. Another effective strategy that can be practiced at home is teaching and reinforcing emotional intelligence. The definition of emotional intelligence is the recognition and understanding of one's thoughts and emotions and how they may impact the thoughts and emotions of others.

Two crucial aspects of developing emotional intelligence are cultivating self-awareness and empathy. Self-awareness enables children to assess their strengths and limitations, and empathy helps them take the perspective of others and imagine how they might feel in a particular situation.

Emotional intelligence cannot be developed passively by watching demonstrations on a screen or by reading a book. To build this complex skill, ongoing practice and reinforcement is needed. Furthermore, your child must be able to adopt the following mentality:

- acknowledging and accepting that he or she is their own person and has a separate identity from other individuals

- acknowledging and accepting that other people can and are allowed to think and feel differently from them (i.e., recognizing that other people's opinions are not an attack on their opinions)

- the ability to relate to universal emotions that are shared among people, such as the feelings of sadness, disappointment, happiness, surprise, and anger

- the ability to watch a social interaction play out and imagine how the individuals involved might be feeling, as well as how they would feel if they were placed in a similar situation

- the ability to imagine the best approach or solution to social situations, taking into consideration how the parties involved would be emotionally impacted by the outcome

Simple ways to help your child adopt the aforementioned mentality are to practice role-playing together, pause and correct their behaviors, and offer rewards and incentives for remembering to take the appropriate action. Provide regular constructive feedback so that your child is aware of what they are doing well and areas for improvement.

It may be helpful to limit screen time during this period and encourage more offline social interactions through after-school programs, social groups, and side hobbies. Exposing your child to people from different social and cultural backgrounds can provide a teachable moment, allowing them to appreciate the diversity of opinions, beliefs, behaviors, and lifestyles. Great ways to expose your child to different people are to enroll them in a volunteer program, work internship, or summer job (for older teens).

Practical Ways to Model Empathy to Your Child

Modeling empathy means adjusting your parental behaviors and attitudes to show compassion toward your child and family members. Doing this can help your child understand what healthy, considerate, and cooperative relationships look like. Since children are highly impressionable, how you talk and act around them becomes their blueprint for engaging with others.

Showing strong emotional regulation and a high regard for the feelings of others enables your child to do the same. Some of the positive habits you can adopt to create a culture of empathy in your home are outlined below.

Pay Attention When Your Child Is Speaking

Whenever your child is speaking to you, pause whatever you are doing and pay attention to them. Shift your body toward them and maintain eye contact to show interest in what they are saying. When you are speaking to your child, set the same expectations. Ask them to pause their video game or show and turn toward you. When spending quality time as a family, put your phones away so that there aren't any distractions in the way.

Talk Through Difficult Emotions

When you are upset or overwhelmed, let those around you know how you are feeling and what you need. This allows you to show vulnerability and get the support you deserve from your family. It can also keep the lines of communication open and clarify misunderstandings so that nobody jumps to conclusions. For example, you might say "I had a stressful day at work today; can I have 15 minutes alone to relax?" or "I feel unheard in this conversation, can we revisit it later?"

Apologize When You Are Wrong

Parents make mistakes and behave inappropriately too. This is important for your child to understand. Essentially, nobody is perfect, and sometimes, people act out of character due to stress and other factors.

Be humble enough to apologize to your child when you have made poor decisions or have hurt them unintentionally. Making excuses for your behavior or pretending as though nothing happened invalidates your child's feelings. Over time, they may lose respect for you and for themselves, believing that it's okay for people to mistreat them and not be held accountable.

Validate Your Child's Experiences

Being born and raised in a different generation from your child means that, sometimes, you might struggle to understand where they are coming from. Their beliefs and lifestyle choices may seem impractical to you because of the different social norms and expectations that were enforced when you were their age.

Displaying emotional intelligence means that you recognize your child's individuality and don't force them to think like you or respond to situations the same way you would. Their understanding of the world is not "wrong" just because it's different from your understanding of the world. To foster a strong bond with your child, practice validating their experiences without imposing your beliefs. Allow them to build skills and knowledge in a way that makes sense to them.

Moreover, remind yourself that you don't have to approve of every decision your child makes to continue supporting them and offering guidance. Your child will inevitably disappoint you (as will many people in your life), but remember that their purpose in life is not to make you happy but instead to evolve into a happier, healthier, and wiser version of themselves.

Taking the lead in teaching and reinforcing social skills at home can improve the nature and quality of your child's relationships with others. When your child's relationships improve, they will feel more confident and comfortable in who they are and gain the courage to take risks and pursue their goals.

Part 3:

Preventative Measures for

Technology Usage

Chapter 6:

Creating Healthy Screen Habits at Home

If your family has gotten used to having devices at the table, it can be difficult to break the cycle... Find a starting point that works for you and use it as an opportunity to reset the relationship between meals and devices.
–Thatcher Wine

Managing Technology at Home

In the previous chapters, we spent time diagnosing technology dependency, uncovering the various ways in which too much screen time can harm your child's cognitive, physical, and psychological well-being. We are now ready to move ahead and discuss proactive ways to manage screen time and prevent these dire consequences. Developing healthy screen habits is the most effective way to reduce and set limits on how often your child is exposed to screens, striking a good balance between online and offline experiences. However, since your child's behaviors are, to some extent, influenced by their home environment, the whole family needs to reassess their relationship with technology and be willing to change their screen habits, too.

Children may not speak often, but they are observant. They watch how their parents communicate, what they do during free time, how they cope with stress, and many other situations. When screens form a big component of parents' lives from the time they wake up to the time they go to bed, children learn that it's normal to spend hours watching TV, playing videos, or scrolling through social media.

Moreover, children learn the value of technology by watching how often their parents make it available. For example, if it is part of a toddler's routine to watch cartoons whenever their parent is busy with house chores like cooking and cleaning, they may grow a strong attachment to TV screens and feel anxious when that aspect of their day is interrupted. Another example is when a parent responds to their child's tantrums or boredom by giving them access to online entertainment via their tablet, computer, or smartphone. Eventually, the child may use technology as a soothing pacifier whenever they are uncomfortable, instead of learning effective ways to process their emotions.

Self-reflection is crucial when thinking about the role and impact of technology on your family life. Consider how much time you spend online on an average day, including when you are at work. Think about how many times some element of technology is incorporated into daily tasks such as driving, shopping, exercising, making financial transactions, reading, staying in touch with friends and family, staying informed with current affairs, and entertaining yourself or relaxing. You may find that nearly every daily task has a digital component, which means that you are "online" for most of the day.

If it is so difficult for you to establish healthy screen time boundaries, imagine how much harder it must be for your child. Essentially, both adults and children are faced with the same challenge of renegotiating the role and influence of technology in their lives. Your child's addiction may be to video games, but yours may be spending hours watching news channels or browsing social media. The common enemy is the invasive technology that threatens family bonds and leads to a breakdown of communication.

Of course, this doesn't mean that screens should be removed at home. With the proper structure and guidelines, technology can enhance your family life and enable you to make memories, such as having movie nights on Fridays or taking photos and videos of your loved ones and creating a digital album or posting on social media. The internet can also provide ideas for family meals, travel destinations, cleaning hacks, family bonding activities, and other useful ways to strengthen your family's well-being.

Sometimes, when you are unavailable to assist your child with homework or don't have the answers to subject-related questions, you can direct them to search engines or AI-powered tools that can offer support. Through online learning, your child can obtain new skills and knowledge, and find mentors or peers who serve as positive role models in their life.

Technology becomes harmful only when there aren't parameters put in place to control what media content your family is exposed to and how often everyone uses their electronic devices. The purpose of the family media plan is to set rules and standards for how your family as a whole interacts with technology. Bear in mind that these rules and standards apply to all family members from the youngest to the oldest. Your family media plan can be as minimalistic as writing a list of technology rules on a page or as comprehensive as creating a booklet that everyone can refer to.

Whether you choose to make a list or a booklet, the family media plan should be seen as a working document that is continuously updated to stay relevant. Additionally, seek your family members' input when compiling the plan to ensure that the rules reflect your shared values.

How to Build a Family Media Plan

One of the factors that can lead to you creating a family media plan is the growing concern about your child's technology usage. However, family media plans aren't solely designed to be a response to poor screen time habits. They can be proactive ways to start a conversation about technology and ensure that everyone understands its function at home and feels empowered to use it within the established boundaries.

Family media plans can also be a great way to teach young children self-control and discipline, encouraging them to reflect on their technology behaviors and correct them on their own. They are beneficial to older children, too, as they encourage them to take ownership of their time and learn how to create productive and balanced routines that accommodate time for family, friends, school, and leisure. Therefore, don't wait until you notice technology dependency or addiction before you introduce the family media plan. There are no strict rules to building a family media plan, but with that said, here are some guidelines that can enhance the structure of your family media plan. Remember to involve your family members when completing these steps so that they can share ideas and feel included during the process.

Identify Your Family Values

Before you start creating the family media plan, identify your family values. These are the principles that keep your family strong and moving in the right direction. If your child is young, these values reflect the ideas and beliefs that you have. However, if your child has reached an age where they can express their thoughts and feelings, their ideas and interests must be considered when establishing family values.

In essence, family values embody your shared vision and mission that informs how you interact with each other, how support is shown, how family bonding time is spent, the type of goals you strive for as a family, and how you interact with people outside of your family and the world around you. To identify your family values and create a mission statement, follow the below guidelines.

Step 1: Brainstorm a List of Values

On a piece of paper, write down a list of principles that you believe are important for maintaining a strong and united family. If you have a partner or spouse, they can create their own list, and then when you are both done, discuss what you have written. Circle the values that appeared on both of your lists and write them down on a separate list. If any of you feel strongly about a value that only appeared on one list, discuss the value again and try to reach a compromise. Keep your family as the main focus of your discussions. Here is a sample list that you can refer to for inspiration:

- hard work

- respect

- trust

- collaboration

- love

- honesty

- open communication

- faith

- adventure

- continuous learning

- patience

- gratitude

- positivity

- support

- discipline

- achievement

- kindness

- responsibility

- forgiveness

- perseverance

Step 2: Review the Values With Your Family

Once you have consolidated your list of values, invite your older child or children to join the discussion. If your child or children aren't old enough to participate in the discussion, spend time reviewing the values by yourself or with your partner or spouse. What's important at this stage is connecting to the "why" behind each value to determine if there is a strong connection with your family. Some values look good on paper but may not be things that motivate your family.

Here are important questions to reflect on and discuss when completing your review:

1. What are our strengths as a family?

2. What activities make us come together as a family?

3. When are we most satisfied as a family?

4. What quote or saying best captures who we are as a family?

5. How do we want to be remembered as a family?

6. How can we support each other as a family?

Step 3: Create a Mission Statement

After completing the review of your values, narrow down your list to 3–7 of your top values. Keeping your list short makes it easy for your family members to recall and incorporate all of the values in their daily lives. Once you have identified your core values, create a mission statement to bring them together. You can use an AI-powered tool to generate a mission statement based on your top values.

Consider the following examples of family mission statements sourced from Bruce Feiler's book *The Secrets of Happy Families* (Feiler, 2013, p. 320):

- Example 1: *The Mission of our family is to create a nurturing place of faith, order, truth, love, happiness, and relaxation, and to provide opportunity for each individual to become responsibly independent, and effectively interdependent, to serve worthy purposes in society.*

- Example 2: *The purpose of our lives is to contribute our unique, God-given gifts to have an extraordinarily positive impact on the lives of others and the world.*

  o *Faith: We pursue our journey with God.*

  o *Family: We love, respect, and are loyal to one another, and build family traditions.*

  o *Attitude: We are grateful, forgiving, optimistic, and polite.*

  o *Health: We make good decisions about how we treat our minds and bodies.*

  o *Knowledge: We celebrate intellectual curiosity and invention.*

  o *Purpose: We purpose our gifts with passion, courage, and perseverance.*

  o *Ownership: We take full responsibility for the planning, actions, and consequences of our decisions and resources.*

  o *Experience: We create a life of adventure and choose experiences over things.*

  o *Justice: We seek to serve and defend others with generosity and without judgment.*

o *Stewardship: We preserve and respect the environment and animals that contribute to our lives.*

Step 4: Reflect on the Role and Impact of Technology on Your Family

After identifying your core values and drafting a mission statement, think about whether your current technology habits support your values. How does technology bring you closer or create distance? How much do you rely on technology versus relying on each other? It's worth mentioning again that technology isn't necessarily bad for families, but without boundaries, it can be harmful.

Discuss the following questions with your spouse and older children to start a constructive conversation about technology and the impact it has on your family life:

1. What online activities do we normally perform at home?

2. How often do we spend time together without electronic devices?

3. Have we managed to strike a balance between online and offline activities?

4. What have been some of the advantages of being online at home?

5. What have been some of the disadvantages of being online at home?

6. When should we be allowed to use our electronic devices, and when shouldn't we?

7. How can we build routines (i.e., morning and nighttime routines) that don't require being online?

8. What family rituals and bonding activities can we introduce to enjoy screen-free entertainment?

Write down the answers to these questions on paper and use them to create the basic rules of your family media plan.

Step 5: Compile Your Family Media Plan

Putting together a family media plan becomes simple once you have identified your family values and understand the role and impact of technology on your family life. The only thing left to do is to create the rules that every member of your family will follow. The rules can be written in a long list or divided into categories. Below are some categories that you might wish to include in your family media plan.

N.B.: Please note that a family media plan template has been provided for your convenience in Part 5 of this book.

Privacy and Safety

Establish rules regarding online safety and protecting sensitive information. For example, you might expect your older child to create secure passwords for all their devices and share them with you, as well as notify you before they decide to change their passwords. Other rules that you might put in place could be:

- **Parental monitoring:** Explain to your child that you will be randomly but regularly monitoring their technology usage, social media posting, or text messages between friends through a tracking tool to keep them safe and ensure that they are conducting themselves appropriately online.

- **Sharing information:** Let your child know what type of information they can share with friends or post online and what information is strictly off-limits. For instance, they might not be allowed to share their current location, identity number, banking details, passwords, or revealing photos of themselves.

- **Approving content:** If your child is below the age of 16, you might require them to ask for approval before watching certain shows, downloading certain apps, playing certain video games, or posting images or videos of themselves.

Screen Usage and Screen-Free Times

An important element of your family media plan is setting expectations around screen usage and screen-free times. For instance, you might list the type of devices your child can use on weekdays and weekends (e.g., video games might only be allowed on weekends).

Additionally, you might set conditions for screen usage, such as only watching TV after completing chores. Lastly, you can set specific times during the day when your child has access to devices and when they don't.

You may also designate rooms or areas around the house where devices are not allowed to enter. These could be the dining room where you enjoy meals together, the study room or section where homework is completed, bedrooms (after a certain time), or the formal sitting room.

Technology Etiquette

Family members need to mind their manners when using technology to ensure that they remain respectful of those around them.

For instance, you might expect your child to excuse themselves and step aside when answering calls or to put their phone away or face down when they are in a group setting. In-person interactions and communication must be prioritized over responding to texts.

Other rules you might put in place may include:

- Use proper greetings and language when writing emails.

- Do not use any profanities or make inappropriate jokes when texting friends.

- Do not share other people's images, videos, or take screenshots of their text messages without asking for permission.

- Do not share or repost content that can be considered offensive or discriminatory.

- Be respectful when talking to adults or setting appointments on the phone.

Your child may be curious to know why these rules are important to follow. Make sure you are prepared to answer them, providing factual information that helps them gain a deeper understanding. Some rules may not be self-explanatory and will require examples and role-playing to make them clear and practical.

Even though this is only a plan with a set of guidelines, you can enforce it as part of the household rules. This means that going against the guidelines will be considered as violating the household rules, and the appropriate disciplinary steps will be followed.

Encouraging Healthy Screen Limits

To ensure the success of your family media plan, setting healthy screen limits is crucial. Ideally, your family members need to know when to go online and when to log off and enjoy offline activities.

Enforcing healthy screen limits is easier the younger your child is. They can tolerate changes to their schedule and quickly adapt to the new routine. However, older children tend to have their preferences on what to watch and when to watch their shows. Convincing them to reduce their screen time could lead to tantrums or pushback. Below are tips that can help you set screen limits at home with minimal confrontation.

Lead by Example

Prioritize face-to-face interactions with your family. For instance, instead of texting your child to come downstairs, go to their room and call them. During free time, find a screen-free activity to do with your child, preferably one that takes you outside. Introduce a bowl where everyone can leave their smartphones during screen-free times. Make sure your smartphone is included.

Encourage Alternative Activities

Train your child to think of screens as the last option after they have gone through a list of alternative activities. Create a chart of fun and stimulating screen-free activities that your child can play indoors and outdoors. Purchase books, art supplies, board games, dress-up costumes, toy furniture, and sports equipment that can keep your child busy for hours. It can also be useful to hide electronic devices so that your child isn't tempted to use them.

Limit the number of TVs in the house to create more screen-free zones.

Monitor Screen Use

Using screen monitoring tools can be a great way to help your older child reflect on their screen habits. You can track the devices they use and how much time they spend on them. Present this information to your child and establish small achievable goals such as working toward reducing social media browsing by 15 minutes each day. Hold your child accountable to their goals, and find ways to reward them and celebrate reaching milestones.

It's not always necessary to use force when setting screen limits. Sometimes, having open discussions, making compromises, and leading by example can positively influence your child's technology behaviors. Make sure that your child feels supported and knows they are not the only ones making changes. Every member of the family is going through the same process of reassessing their relationship with technology.

Chapter 7:

Building Screen-Free Routines

We remember only what we pay attention to. When we decide what to pay attention to in the moment, we are making a broader decision about how we want to spend our lives. –Catherine Price

Daily Schedules and Routines

Young children do not have the willpower to create a structured routine for themselves. They depend on the rules enforced at home, consistent daily routines, and communicated boundaries to change their behaviors. A 10-year-old won't remember or feel motivated to regulate their video game use unless there are strict measures put in place to limit their device usage. These strict measures aren't meant to punish the child but to teach them responsible behaviors. It's up to parents to create a home environment that promotes offline activities and provides enough structure to allow children to stay productive throughout the day. Daily schedules and routines make your child's day predictable. This may sound boring to you, however, growing children need stability and consistency to regulate their emotions, manage stress and anxiety, and feel confident exploring the world. Schedules and routines make your child's home and school environment feel safe and nurturing. As a result, their minds are more relaxed and conducive to learning and building healthy relationships.

Another benefit of daily schedules and routines is that you have more control over your child's daily tasks and activities. Instead of giving them free rein to entertain themselves and do as they please, you can schedule healthy tasks that are stimulating, educational, and creative. Your schedules can be designed in such a way that they reduce screen time and promote enriching offline activities.

Young children do not understand enough about their daily schedule to give their input. However, older children may want to be involved in the process of creating their routines. You may disagree with each other on which tasks are important or unimportant or how much time they get to relax versus doing something productive. Be open to receiving your child's suggestions and creating a schedule that both of you feel comfortable with. Some tasks can be negotiated in terms of frequency or duration, but make your nonnegotiables clear from the get-go.

For example, your teenage daughter may be against the idea of browsing social media in the evenings because they want some form of online interaction with their friends during the day. To accommodate their needs, you might be clear about your nonnegotiable, which is sticking to two hours of social media browsing per day, but give them the freedom to break up the two hours into smaller time slots from the time they get back at school. This way, both of your expectations are met.

Making changes to preexisting schedules and routines is a matter that you need to discuss with your child before putting them into effect. Many children find transitions and sudden changes stressful and may likely respond adversely to the new expectations. For example, if you are considering reducing your child's screen time or withholding certain devices during the week, introduce them to the change gradually. Start by discussing your wishes with them first and explain why these changes are important. Help them understand your concerns and the long-term impact of continuing the current screen habits. Ease them into this new routine so that they are aware of the behaviors expected of them

Moreover, give them an idea of what to expect by drawing a picture or diagram, creating a chart with the new schedule, or presenting hypothetical scenarios. Encourage your child to ask questions and voice their fears or frustrations. See how you can compromise to address some of their needs, but make your nonnegotiable rules clear. You can also create a trial period where you test out the new schedule or routine and get feedback from your child before implementing it permanently.

The Components of Healthy and Balanced Schedules

You may be wondering what it takes to establish a well-rounded and healthy schedule. The answer is just four elements: routines, transitions, outdoor time, and free-choice time. Here is an overview of the elements and ways you can incorporate them into your child's schedule.

Routines

When creating a schedule, start by writing down a list of daily tasks that your child needs to complete and the order in which they need to complete them. This arrangement of daily tasks is called a routine. You can include several routines during the day to help organize your child's tasks better. For instance, you might create a morning routine, homework routine, house chores routine, and bedtime routine. Each of these routines consists of a list of tasks that your child completes every day.

Effective routines are simple and easy to understand and follow. Younger children may benefit from having a visual aid such as a chart with pictures to memorize their routines. Older children may prefer using calendars or productivity apps to manage their routines independently.

Transitions

Preschoolers and elementary-aged children may need some time to mentally adjust before completing the next task on their schedules. This short period of rest and adjustment is called a transition. Children typically don't respond well when they are told to stop what they are doing and start another task, especially when they are enjoying the task at hand. It's therefore crucial to plan for your transitions and have a strategy for how you are going to gently turn your child's focus to something else.

One effective strategy is to offer several warnings through a countdown before your child needs to make a transition. You can also place a stopwatch next to them so they can see how much time they have left. Another way to manage transitions is to distract your child with a fun and active task that gets them out of their seat. Movement can help your child release tension and feel relaxed and alert for the next task.

For example, after playing outside, bring your child inside for light and slow stretches before they shift to a quiet task like reading or completing schoolwork.

Outdoor Time

Outdoor time is as important for young children as it is for older children. The benefits of being outdoors are numerous, such as getting Vitamin D exposure through sunlight, engaging in light or moderate physical activity, and spending time away from screens. Outdoor time is unstructured, meaning that your child gets to choose what activities they would like to do. However, you can provide a list of healthy options for them to choose from. Consider your child's interests and hobbies when creating the list to ensure they are enthusiastic about going outside. Another way to motivate them is by making the necessary materials and equipment for activities available. For example, to encourage your child to paint, purchase art supplies. If you want them to play sports, make sure they have the right gear and equipment.

Free-Choice Time

Free-choice time is an opportunity during the day when your child gets to play. Similar to outdoor time, this period of the day is unstructured. How your child chooses to play is up to them; however, you can set some ground rules. For example, it's normal for your child to reach out for their gadgets during free-choice time, but to monitor their usage, you can set screen limits. You can also enforce technology breaks after every show watched to balance online and offline activities during free-choice time. Even though this part of your child's day won't always be productive, it can provide relaxation and entertainment, two essential needs for a balanced lifestyle.

Take a moment to think about your child's current schedule. Do you have routines in place to help your child get through daily tasks like homework and house chores? Have you thought about ways to manage transitions to avoid emotional outbursts and defensiveness?

Does your child get sufficient time to spend outdoors and time to play? These are all crucial elements that are needed to improve your child's schedule, reduce screen dependency, and set them up for success. For ideas of screen-free routines that you can adopt or customize, head over to Part 5 of the book.

Helping Your Child Improve Their Time Management

Part of the reason why children spend too much time on their screens is that they don't have proper time management. As such, they end up glued to their devices for hours, not realizing how much of their day is being spent unproductively. Time management is about recognizing the value of your time and planning your day accordingly.

Time is the rarest commodity in the world because once it's spent, it cannot be brought back. Wasting a day may not have drastic implications on your child's home and school life, but when several wasted days turn to wasted weeks and months, they can find themselves falling behind their peers and struggling to achieve their goals.

Instructing your child on how to manage their time may be doable when they are young, but an older child is expected to have developed this skill already. With age comes greater responsibilities and demands, such as maintaining good grades, studying for difficult tests, making time for socializing and self-care, and setting goals for life after high school.

Without effective time management skills, your child may find their schedule overwhelming and instead of being proactive, they might turn to mind-numbing distractions like TV, video games, or social media. Ultimately, you cannot control the type of stressors your child is faced with. Nevertheless, you can help them improve their time management so that they feel in control of their time and know how to make the most of the time they are given. Here are a few time management strategies to discuss with and teach your child.

Start With Realistic Goals and Expectations

There are only a handful of tasks that you can squeeze into a 24-hour day. Attempting to fill each hour of your day with activity can be counterproductive. If your child attends school, they only have a few hours in the afternoon to complete homework, house chores, and enjoy free time before they eat dinner and prepare for bed. Therefore, encourage your child to think realistically about what they can achieve in a day.

For instance, starting and completing a science project in one day is possible, but how much time would that take? And what other tasks would they need to forfeit to achieve this? Some tasks may require several hours to complete or ongoing practice (if they are learning a sport or skill), and may need to be broken down into smaller manageable chunks and spread across several weeks.

For example, when your child spaces out their learning for an upcoming exam, they can study for 30 minutes per day over 2 weeks instead of cramming hours' worth of studying 2–3 days before the exam.

Teach your child the SMART goal-setting method to help them set realistic goals for how to manage their time. SMART outlines criteria for crafting goals to make them practical. Your child can focus on setting goals that are specific (easy to understand and take action on), measurable (include a useful metric to track progress), achievable (require resources that your child already has available), relevant (aligned to your child's interests and desires), and time-bound (can be completed within a reasonable time frame).

Here is an example of a SMART goal: *To practice a list of math sums for 30 minutes, on Monday and Wednesday afternoons, so that I can improve my math average by 5%–10% at the end of the semester.*

Decide What Tasks Take Priority

Not every task that appears to be urgent is worth your time. Prioritization is a core aspect of time management because it allows you to identify tasks and activities that provide the most value and start with them.

Procrastination is a common behavior among adults and children. It occurs whenever we delay taking action on important tasks. We may be confused about which tasks to start with and end up doing nothing constructive with our time. By teaching your child to prioritize their daily tasks, they can create and follow an agenda rather than "going with the flow."

A simple way to teach your child how to prioritize tasks is to introduce them to the 80/20 rule. This rule suggests that 80% of your child's productivity comes as a result of 20% of the work done (Kattoor, 2023). If they had 10 tasks to complete in a day, only 2 of them would be considered high value (tasks that help contribute toward achieving their goals or maintaining good habits). To practice the 80/20 rule, help your child create a to-do list and go through the tasks, evaluating which ones fall under the "20% category." Those are the tasks your child needs to start with.

Create Designated Areas for Specific Tasks at Home

The human brain processes information like a computer. The more organized the data is, the easier the processing becomes and the less likely the brain is to crash. Having designated spaces for specific tasks at home can improve your child's focus and motivation. Whenever they step into a specific space, their brain is mentally prepared for whatever task that will be performed there. This also means that some parts of your child's brain get some rest when they enter certain areas of the home where their expertise isn't needed.

For example, creating a designated study office or room where your child goes to complete their homework helps their prefrontal cortex (the region of the brain responsible for logic and learning) wake up. After their homework session, they may retreat to the playroom where there aren't any school-related learning materials in sight and their prefrontal cortex can rest temporarily while their amygdala and hippocampus (two regions that promote creativity and imagination) take center stage. Engaging these different parts of the brain, one at a time, reduces mental exhaustion and ensures that your child is developing a variety of skills and knowledge.

In addition to this, you can consider creating a designated "technology room" where the whole family has access to screens and different electronic devices. Keeping your devices in one area of the home helps your child avoid the temptation to engage with technology. Their brain also learns to only "shut down" when they are spending time in that specific room.

Encourage Regular Breaks

Lastly, you can help your child improve their time management by encouraging them to take regular breaks during and in between tasks. Breaks should not be seen as a waste of time. Instead, see them as windows for your child's brain to process the information it has absorbed. Staying with the computer analogy, the last thing you want is for your child's brain to overheat due to chronic use. After intense periods of focus, get your child to stand up and take a walk, stretch their legs, grab a snack from the kitchen, and reflect on what they have learned.

Breaks should not be used for going online, but rather for recharging and being present. Additionally, the breaks shouldn't be so long that your child procrastinates and feels unmotivated to continue working. Generally, 5–15 minute break intervals are appropriate depending on the minutes spent in deep focus (i.e., the longer the time spent in deep focus, the longer the break should be).

Creating a Screen Time Reward System

In many households, screens are a free-for-all for children, meaning they are accessible whenever. Over time, this can lead to entitlement. For example, a preschooler with access to a tablet may feel entitled to it several times a day, including times when being on screens is inappropriate like bath time or meal times. A preteen who has recently bought a smartphone may feel entitled to use their phone at home, school, during family bonding time, and until late hours of the night.

To improve your child's relationship with technology, teach them that they aren't entitled to screens because too much exposure can be harmful to them. You can compare it to eating a bowl of ice cream every day; eventually, what was supposed to be a rewarding experience becomes dangerous for their health. Screen time should therefore be seen as a privilege, a special right that is given to them whenever they have earned it.

The concept of "earning" screen time may sound strange to a child who has never had to do anything to binge on their shows. However, emphasize the fact that anything worthwhile in life is earned and the prize is always worth the sacrifices.

So, how can your child earn screen time? Start by thinking about all of the tasks that are essential for their physical and emotional development, such as taking showers every morning, eating a balanced diet, reading, playing outside, being a team player at home by doing chores, making an effort to bond with friends and family, going to sleep on time, and so on. Performing these tasks consistently (daily) may earn your child screen time.

Another way to structure your screen time reward system is to think of troublesome behaviors you would like your child to unlearn, such as procrastination, back talking, throwing tantrums, poor time management or organization skills, or a lazy approach to completing schoolwork. To earn screen time, they would need to show a consistent track record of not displaying these behaviors, or at least reduce the frequency of these behaviors (e.g., two incidents of procrastination instead of it being a daily issue).

If you cannot think of tasks your child can perform to earn screen time, ask them to propose ideas. For example, you could say, "I know it's Friday night and you want to stay up 20 minutes longer to continue playing video games. What can you do tomorrow to make up for this additional screen time?" Hear what they have to say and reach a compromise. Make sure the task they propose is worthy of the privilege. For example, taking the dog for a walk, mowing the lawn, cooking dinner, or cleaning their bedroom are tasks that require effort and qualify them for screen time. Keep reminding yourself that the purpose isn't to punish your child but to help them learn successful habits.

Lastly, if screen time is being used in your household as a reward, refrain from using it as a consequence as well. Not only can doing this discourage your child from working hard to earn screen time, but it can also put them off from embracing technology. Once earned, screen time shouldn't be taken away or withheld, even if your child misbehaves shortly after rewarding them. Allow them to enjoy their reward, but take note of their behavior and let them know that you are closely monitoring them.

For example, you might say, "Your behavior as of late is worrying and we may need to find ways to correct it before you can get back to using social media."

In Part 5, you will find a simple screen time reward checklist that you can customize and use to motivate your child to develop healthy habits at home.

Chapter 8:

Parental Role Modeling

Electronics and technology have a way of clouding our vision for the people sitting next to us. Uncloud your life, look around. Be present. —Eric Overby

Leading by Example

Sara Foss, a writer, shared a story a while ago about the time she realized she was hooked on her screens (Foss, 2023). She became concerned about her five-year-old son's growing interest in technology and how that could potentially spiral into full-blown obsession several months or years down the line. However, just as she was analyzing her son's screen behaviors, she couldn't help but reflect on her technology consumption as well. She recalled how, when her son was only months old, he would be playing next to her while she worked on her laptop or surfed the net. This became a normal way for them to spend time together. Technology was the "third wheel" getting in the way of true bonding. But what was more disturbing was that her son had learned that being chronically online was okay.

It's common for parents to notice unhealthy screen habits in their children, but how many parents go deeper and reflect on how their own actions may, to some extent, influence their children's behaviors? This doesn't mean that parents are to blame for their children's improper behaviors—however, they do have some degree of power, control, and agency to determine the quality of their children's home environment.

Bonnie Harris, the Director of Connective Parenting—a coaching and counseling service for parents—has this to say about children's screen addictions: "My whole focus is in switching the perception of parents from 'my child is being a problem' to 'my child is having a problem.' I think screen time is one of those issues that is symptomatic of things that are going on inside the family" (Harris, n.d.). In essence, children's screen habits can be the result of how much time children spend alone or entertaining themselves versus bonding with their parents and forming social relationships. It can also be the result of ineffective parenting techniques, weak rules and boundaries, or the lack of a strong culture and value system that families follow and hold themselves accountable to.

Whenever you notice troublesome behavior in your child, such as excessive screen use, stop and think to yourself: *My child is having a problem.* Certain physical, mental, and emotional needs are going unnoticed and their behavior may be a coping mechanism to address those needs. This doesn't make you a bad parent; rather, see it as a wake-up call to pay more attention to your child and lead by example. If certain habits about your child irk you, consider what unmet needs those habits might be soothing, and through your actions (not lectures), show your child positive alternatives for fulfilling those needs.

For example, suppose your teenage daughter is obsessed with social media and staying connected with her virtual friends. Over time, this has made her self-centered and out of touch with reality. But what unmet needs could be behind this self-destructive habit? Depending on your daughter's life circumstances, her chronic use of social media could be filling the following inner holes:

- the need for reassurance and validation (to be told that she is smart, beautiful, and capable)

- the need for emotional connection and belonging (the desire for a sense of family and community in the absence of real-life, supportive friendships and family ties)

- the need for identity exploration and self-expression (to experience the freedom of being authentically herself in response to her real-life controlled and restrictive environment)

- the need for distraction and avoiding negative emotions (to temporarily distract her mind from ongoing stress or conflict that is occurring in her life)

Now that you are aware of what your daughter's problem might be, you can work on becoming a good example of how to face these common challenges with positive coping strategies.

Remember, *show, don't tell*. Show your daughter, through your actions, alternative ways to fulfill these needs without relying on screens. For example, you might practice positive affirmations, set aspirational goals, and celebrate your achievements to teach your daughter healthy ways of validating herself. Or you might spend time investing in your social life and expanding your support network to show your daughter the value of social connections.

In some cases, you may need to modify your parenting approach to be more accommodating of your child's needs. For instance, if your daughter is looking to social media for validation, there's an opportunity for you to offer more words of encouragement and praise. If she needs social media to distract herself from ongoing family or school stress, perhaps you can work on opening the lines of communication and strengthening trust with your daughter so she feels safe speaking to you about her troubling thoughts and feelings. If your daughter feels more freedom being herself online than she does offline, this could be a sign that your home environment has become too strict, critical, and judgmental. Work on being more tolerant of your daughter's beliefs, choices, and personality without directly or indirectly pushing her to be someone she is not.

Healthy Screen Habits Parents Can Adopt

The important message that you must seek to get across to your child is that technology isn't harmful when it is used responsibly. Since actions are louder words, work on developing healthy screen habits that show your child how to build a positive relationship with technology. Below are some suggestions you can try.

Find Screen-Free Ways to Entertain Yourself

Your child may be used to seeing you busy with tasks around the house, but whenever you have free time, find a screen-free activity to help you unwind or keep you entertained. This could be gardening, reading a book, going for a walk, spending time in prayer, or having meaningful conversations with friends and family. Moreover, consider making most of your family bonding activities screen-free to allow for uninterrupted quality time.

Prioritize People Over Gadgets

Technology tends to make us antisocial. Whenever we are looking down at our smartphones or watching something on TV, we struggle to listen and pay attention to the people around us. Teach your child to always prioritize human connection and communication by making your gadgets secondary. Whenever your child enters the room, put down your smartphone and turn toward them. If you are receiving a call or text message but your child needs your attention, respond to them first. If you are watching television and your child asks a question, pause the show or lower the volume so that you can focus on what they are saying.

Have a Purpose for Using Screens

Find a compelling reason for using technology so that you don't find yourself mindlessly surfing the internet. For example, you might be using technology for research purposes, brainstorming ideas, planning special events, organizing your tasks, tracking your fitness, meditating, and so on. Once your screens have served their purpose, unplug and get back to the real world. This habit teaches your child to use electronic devices with clear intentions rather than curbing boredom.

Avoid Carrying Your Devices With You Around the House

When we are out in public, we are forced to keep our tech gadgets near to us so that people can reach people and be accessible. However, in the comfort of our homes, we don't need to be constantly online and accessible. To encourage your child to take breaks from technology, create a communal charging station and "parking spot" for your smartphones and other devices. As soon as you enter the house after work or after running errands, leave your gadgets in that area and continue your house tasks. If you need to be reachable at home, consider taking your devices out for brief periods and putting them back in the spot. In the evenings, encourage all of your family members to return their devices to the charging station instead of going to bed with them.

A Parent's Guide to Overcoming Screen Addiction

Modeling healthy screen habits in front of your child is hard when you are struggling with a screen addiction. As mentioned in Chapter 1 of the book, screen addiction is a mental disease that develops after a lengthy period of screen dependency, where you feel you cannot function at your best without using technology. Accepting that you may be addicted to technology isn't easy due to how normalized being chronically online has become.

Breaking away from technology requires intentional effort; otherwise, you may find yourself enjoying its conveniences too much. Think about how popular remote jobs have become over the years. The concept of working from home sounds like the ideal work arrangement on paper. However, when you consider just how many hours of your day you would need to spend in front of a screen, on video or voice calls, and sometimes staying "online" after work hours, you can see how unhealthy screen habits can emerge.

Another invention that we all love is the convenience of smartphone apps. Nowadays, you can find an app for virtually any task, including offline activities like reading, walking, and meditating. Don't feel like attending an educational institution? Don't worry, you can enroll in an online course. Don't have the energy to drive to the grocery store? No problem, you can have your groceries delivered to your door. For many of us, our entertainment has also moved online, particularly in this post-

COVID era. Social networking platforms like Meta and X and invite-only communities like Clubhouse host ongoing discussions and trends that can have us entertained for hours. It's therefore not impossible for even adults to develop screen addictions.

You don't need to wait until a serious addiction problem forms to address your unhealthy relationship with technology. By simply acknowledging that you are online too much and may benefit from reducing your screen time, you are reversing the symptoms of screen dependency and addiction. Some of the warning signs to look out for include:

- the inability to spend hours or days away from your electronic devices or certain apps and websites

- obsessively thinking about what you are missing out on (e.g., the videos, TV shows, content, and conversations you are missing out on) when you are offline

- using screens as an emotional blanket when you are feeling angry, sad, lonely, bored, or unmotivated

- lying to your friends and family about how often you scroll through social media, shop online, or play video games out of guilt or shame

- feeling down, anxious, or depressed whenever you put your devices away

- neglecting other aspects of your life such as your health, career, relationships, and goals at the expense of technology

Similar to the discussion we had earlier in the chapter about your child, your unhealthy screen habits could be symptoms of unmet personal needs.

Reflect on the "emotional buzz" that screens provide you, and then think of the areas of your life where that same buzz could be missing. For example, being online might give you a sense of belonging that you don't get from your real-life relationships.

You might know a lot of people in real life but don't feel seen or validated by them. When you go online, you may find strangers who are kind, reassuring, and accepting of who you are. After identifying the area of growth—your relationships— you can set goals to expand your real-life support system and strengthen existing relationships.

Another example is if you feel a sense of satisfaction expressing your views online. Consider how your self-expression may be limited in real life. Maybe you work in a conservative job that doesn't allow you to use your creativity or maybe you grew up in a conservative home where expressing your thoughts and feelings wasn't encouraged.

Being online gives you the freedom to break your silence and express yourself unapologetically. You may also get to be part of creative communities that support this underdeveloped aspect of your identity.

By identifying this area of growth—self-expression—you can set goals to start showing up more authentically in your real life through actions such as letting go of people-pleasing tendencies, validating yourself instead of seeking external validation, and connecting to your hobbies and passions so that your life doesn't revolve around work or family. You won't need the emotional buzz of screens when your life becomes your source of inspiration!

Like any form of addiction, screen addiction is not curable, but it can be treated through medication, therapy, rehabilitation programs, and support groups. Consult a medical doctor if you suspect that you may be living with an undiagnosed addiction.

The Importance of Parenting Involvement

Taking an interest and being involved in your child's screen usage can help them practice healthy screen habits. Essentially, when they know that their screen time is being monitored and certain apps, content, or devices are strictly off-limits, they can overcome the temptation of breaking the rules. However, when they are given free rein to use technology at their discretion, staying disciplined and doing the right thing can be difficult.

Self-control isn't a skill that your child is born with. It must be introduced, instilled, and inspired in your child. Part of teaching them self-control is by setting boundaries early on and making a clear distinction between healthy and unhealthy screen habits. Additionally, you must teach your child how to engage with different electronic devices.

For example, there may be a list of things they can or cannot do on the Internet for their own safety. The Internet is a global village, with over five billion active users browsing daily (Pelchen, 2024). With so many people on there, some older and some younger, your child can easily find themselves caught up with the wrong crowd, viewing violent and graphic content, or developing harmful habits like trolling, spamming, sending or requesting explicit content, or cyberbullying. Thus, you might block certain websites, filter your child's Google searches, or link their email account with yours.

Many social media platforms require children to be 13 years or older to open accounts. However, at that young age, children are still not mature enough to use social media without parental supervision. We know that social media works with algorithms, which are a set of calculations that determine the type of content your child is shown on their feeds. Algorithms can expose your child to inappropriate and violent content based on their search results or the content liked by the people they follow on social media.

To protect your child, you might discuss the possibility of following each other on social media so that you are updated on the content they post and engage with. You might also consider asking them to share their password so you can monitor their account. These measures can be seen as invasive, especially to older children, which is why consent is needed.

Spying on or stalking your child not only undermines the trust you have spent many years building with them but also creates secrecy and a disconnect in your relationship. Respect your child's wishes if they choose to maintain their social media privacy. Trust that you have instilled enough values in them to help them make the right choices on their own. Create an open-door policy where your child can share anything about their online experiences without getting in trouble or being judged.

For example, if they receive a strange text from a social media user, help them understand how to navigate the situation without making them feel guilty for interacting with the stranger.

When it comes to films and TV shows, you can enjoy more control, thanks to television parental guidelines. Every show or movie will have an age group rating to indicate the appropriateness of the content for children of all ages. Some ratings appear on the top left corner of the screen when the TV show begins; while others appear in the description section. If you are ever unsure about the TV rating of a show, simply do a Google search. Here is a list of seven ratings you may come across:

- **TV-Y:** The content is suitable for all children.

- **TV-Y7:** The content is suitable for children 7 years and older.

- **TV-Y7-FV:** The content is suitable for children 7 years and older and includes elements of "fantasy violence" which may cause distress for some children.

- **TV-G:** The content is suitable for both adults and children and doesn't include violent or sexual scenes, or strong language.

- **TV-PG:** This content requires parental supervision because it may consist of themes, scenes, or language that is inappropriate for young viewers.

- **TV-14:** The content is suitable for children 14 years and older, as it contains themes or scenes with violence, strong language, or sexual situations.

- **TV-MA:** The content is for a "mature audience" only, ideally for adults but strictly not for children under 17 years old.

Some TV sets come with built-in features to block shows or channels that are unsuitable for specific age groups. A similar feature can also be found on popular streaming platforms like Netflix where you can control the type of content each profile can can view.

Rating systems are included in video games and smartphone apps, too, thanks to the rating system created by the Entertainment Software Rating Board (ESRB). Here are common ratings you may come across:

- **E:** The video game or app is suitable for everyone (no age restriction).

- **E-10+:** The video game or app is suitable for children 10 years and older. The content may include mildly offensive language, mild violence, and suggestive themes.

- **T:** The video game or app is suitable for teenagers, generally 13 years and older. The content may include violence, crude humor, some blood or gore, acts of gambling, and strong language.

- **M:** The video game or app is suitable for a mature audience only, generally 17 years and older. The content may include intense violence, explicit sexual situations, intense blood and gore, and strong language.

- **AO:** The video game or app is for adults only (in some countries this may be 18 and older and in others 21 and older). Users may be expected to bet or gamble in real life or be exposed to long scenes of violence or sexual content.

- **RP:** The rating on this particular video game or app is still pending.

Another way to monitor your child's screen time is to practice co-viewing. This involves watching a show or movie with your child. What's great about co-viewing is that it can double up as family bonding time. Children five years and below may benefit from co-viewing experiences since Mom or Dad can explain to the child what they are watching or make the show interactive by singing along or following the instructions given by the presenter. Older children may find co-viewing "uncool" and may prefer to have private screen time.

However, you can create family bonding rituals that require watching media together. These can include family movie nights, video game competitions, creating family TikTok videos, listening to podcasts in the car, or having shared music-listening parties.

Co-viewing helps you understand what type of online content your child enjoys so that you learn more about them. It isn't about catching them out or bringing up concerns that you may have. Be happy that your child voluntarily invites you into their digital world and gets excited to share online experiences with you.

Part 4:

Age-Specific Strategies for

Cutting Back on Screen Time

Chapter 9:

Strategies for Toddlers (0–2 years)

Old robots are becoming more human and young humans are becoming more like robots. –Lorin Morgan-Richards

Promoting Early Childhood Learning and Play Without Screens

In the previous section of the book, we looked at various strategies that can help to prevent unhealthy screen habits. When it comes to technology dependency and addiction, prevention is better than cure. Building upon those strategies, this section delves into age-appropriate tips and need-to-know information about managing children's screen time. Each chapter will focus on a specific age group, but take the time to read through all four chapters, since you may gain valuable insights that can improve your approach to technology at home. In this chapter, we are going to discuss tips and tricks for managing screen-free time for children aged 0–2 years old, since no screens are recommended at all. At this stage of your child's development, their brains are a fertile ground for learning. Within the first year, science reveals that their brain will double in size; by the time they turn 3, their brain will have grown to 80% of its full capacity (Happiest Baby Staff, n.d.). This begs the question: What skills, knowledge, and behavior is your child learning?

Studies continue to show that infants and toddlers don't learn much from screens because they can't make sense of what they are watching (Nelson, n.d.). Instead, screen exposure robs them of their brain's potential to build millions of neural connections through stimulating human interactions, offline play, sensory experiences, and being outdoors in nature. To add to this, any form of screen time (except for video chats with loved ones) can lead to attention, memory, and impulse control issues as they get older.

One of the common reasons why parents expose their little ones to screens is that they fear them becoming bored from playing in the playpen, rolling around, or scanning their environment. The mistake here is thinking that babies need as much stimulation as grown adults.

You may feel bored after several hours of silence or carrying out the same routine, day in and day out, for weeks and months on end. However, your child, who is fairly new to the world, finds their mundane "eat-burp-sleep-play" lifestyle safe and nurturing.

Dr. Mona Amin, who is a pediatrician and infant development expert, explains how boredom is a positive sign during early childhood development. Bored children will likely develop a secure attachment style with their parents, she believes, as this means that their environment feels safe and predictable (*Do*

Babies Get Bored? Why a Bored Baby Is a Good Thing, 2024, para. 3). There aren't any sudden changes happening around them that overwhelm their senses and cause stress. Every day feels the same, and their parents' reactions to them are also consistent.

"Excitement" to your infant or toddler is not a vibrant atmosphere with different sounds, bright flashing lights, ongoing movement or commotion, and an endless stream of cartoons. For them, excitement is discovering new ways to move their bodies, form different sounds with their mouths, explore new tastes, and have genuine face-to-face contact with their family members.

Placing different sizes, shapes, and textures of toys in your child's playpen and allowing them to stare, throw, or lick them enhances the following development skills:

- sensory exploration and awareness

- fine motor skills and hand-eye coordination

- cognitive development through cause-and-effect understanding

- spatial awareness and understanding of object permanence

- curiosity and problem-solving skills

- tactile discrimination and texture recognition

- oral motor skills and exploration

- early categorization and comparison skills

- emotional regulation through self-soothing behaviors

- gross motor skills through reaching, grasping, and throwing

Can you see how what may seem to be a boring activity has your child's brain working and learning? In contrast, if you had placed a tablet in front of them with access to different animated content, they would learn the following:

- passive consumption rather than active exploration

- reduced attention span due to constant stimulation

- dependence on external entertainment for engagement

- limited sensory and tactile exploration

- less development of fine motor skills

- diminished problem-solving opportunities

- overexposure to fast-paced visual stimuli

- limited opportunities for creativity and imagination

- potential for delayed language and social skills development

- decreased opportunity for independent play and self-regulation skills

Stimulating your child's brain without screens is easier than you may think. In the next section, you will learn about interactive games and activities that they can play independently or with you.

Interactive Play and Learning Activities That Do Not Involve Screens

It's during the week or weekend, and your infant or toddler has woken up from their nap and is looking up at the ceiling. What can they do to power up their brain? Depending on your child's age and how much they can move around, they have a few different screen-free options.

Creative Free Play

Place safe and age-appropriate toys in your child's hands, above them, or within crawling or walking distance, and allow them to explore the toys. Their brain will get to work trying to process what they are observing, which provides a stimulating experience. If they can use various body parts to play with their toys, your child also gets an opportunity to strengthen their muscles, coordination, balance, spatial recognition, and other important physical skills. The types of toys that are suitable for children at this stage of life include soft stacking toys, building blocks, rubber bath toys, books, balls, rattles, mirrors, teething toys, and musical toys. Baby play mats or chairs with hanging toys can also provide entertainment for your child.

Listening to Books Being Read

Your little one may not be able to speak as of yet, however, their brain is processing new sounds and words every day. Listening to you reading can enhance their speech, tone, and facial recognition, prompting them to mimic you and use their tongue and mouth to form sounds and make faces too. During your child's free time, you can also put books in front of them that they can stare at and flip through. When doing this, they learn how to recognize emotion and positive social interactions.

And even though they cannot read the words on the page, their brain is collecting the data and storing it for later when they start learning vocabulary.

Playing Music

Music has a profound effect on child development. Not only does it encourage your child to pay attention to the jingles or words, but it can also activate their imagination, reduce stress levels, and allow them to engage both the right and left sides of their brain.

Neurologists believe that exposure to music can enhance young children's emotional resilience and problem-solving skills (*Kids & Music*, 2018). For example, one study found that listening to classical music from composers like Mozart for 10 minutes could improve spatial reasoning skills far superior than spending moments in silence or listening to relaxation instructions designed to lower blood pressure (Jenkins, 2001).

Both music with words and without words are beneficial for your child. For instance, nursery rhyme songs can expose your child to new words and allow you to sing along and bond with them. They can also gain the same skills from listening to audiobooks or story time videos.

Exploring the Home

Another way that toddlers create their own fun is by exploring the home. You might know where everything is around the house because you have walked in it and around it several times. However, your child, who is still learning to crawl or walk, feels like they are taking a tour inside a mega shopping mall for the first time. Home exploration is recommended because it keeps your child physically active and provides a unique sensory experience. Please note that there may be some parts of your home that are unsafe for them to enter, such as the garage, home office, staircases, balcony or deck, and fireplaces. Other areas of the home such as the kitchen, living room, bathroom, dining room, or basement can be safe with full-time adult supervision. If you want to keep your child in one secure area without them entering other spaces, consider fencing the area off. Before giving your child the freedom to explore different house objects, remove anything sharp, pointy, delicate, poisonous (if ingested), or flammable.

Validating Your Child's Verbal and Nonverbal Communication

Babies start communicating in the womb by reacting to their mothers' or fathers' voices or showing excitement when they hear laughter, a book being read, or certain music playing (Aggarwal, 2024). Talking back to your child and showing that you acknowledge their attempt at getting your attention may not be something the fetus understands. However, when your child enters the world, they may easily recognize the voices that spoke to them and feel a greater sense of comfort and safety.

Screen exposure during the first two years of your child's life can lead to speech and language delays. This happens because while watching content, your child is not prompted or motivated to speak. They are completely enthralled by the show playing on the screen that sounds and words escape them.

Some of the signs of speech and language delays to look out for between 0–2 years include:

- struggles to repeat a sound made by an adult

- uses gestures like pointing rather than making a sound

- shows no reaction to verbal requests

- only uses a few of the same words to communicate basic needs

Take into consideration that children are unique and not everyone will reach their developmental milestones at the same time. Sometimes, speech and language delays are caused by the child's laid-back personality; they are capable of making sounds and using words and phrases to communicate, but just don't feel inspired to yet. With that said, some delays may reveal more serious issues like hearing problems, autism, or brain impairments. Thus, it's always best to follow the developmental milestone chart and consult your pediatrician the moment you notice any of the signs mentioned above.

Cutting back on screens and providing your child ample opportunities to generate sounds and use words can also be helpful. Children between 0–2 years old communicate through cooing, crying, smiling, making eye contact, moving their bodies, imitating sounds, and stringing together simple phrases (the closer they get to 2 years old). Your job as a parent is to acknowledge their communication, just as you would someone who was trying to get your attention. Think of it this way: If your spouse asked you a question, would you ignore them? Or if your friend made a request, would you think they are being unserious?

Many parents unknowingly dismiss their infants and toddlers when they are communicating because their sounds or nonverbal gestures and facial expressions are not considered "real communication." In reality, these sounds and gestures are the building blocks of fluent speech and expression. Without making them, your child has no way to test whether they are on the right track. Remember that during this crucial stage of their life, their brain is absorbing large amounts of information. They see something, try to make sense of it, then find a category in their brain to file it under. By acknowledging and validating your child's attempts at communication, they receive positive feedback that solidifies the information they are learning. For example, you might notice that your 3-month-old baby keeps looking at your breast or their milk bottle, and you say, "Oh, you must be hungry. It's time for us to eat," then immediately give them milk to drink. Your baby learns that eye contact is an effective way to express their needs. If you only realize they are hungry when they start crying, they might learn that crying gets their needs met.

Or maybe you notice your 18-month-old child pointing at your pet dog in the garden. This could signal two things: They could either be curious about the dog (imagine an older child asking "What's that?") or they may want to be carried to the dog (pointing could be their way of requesting for you to take them outside). Teaching them how to pronounce the word "dog" might satisfy their curiosity. You might approach the dog and say "D-O-G. DOG. Say 'dog,'" while pointing your finger in the same direction. On the other hand, if your child's pointing was a request to go outside, you might open the sliding door and allow them to waddle to the garden. Either way, by being responsive to their communication, they learn that their thoughts and feelings matter.

Another way to encourage your child to communicate is to incorporate dialogue during tasks such as nappy changes, bath time, feeding time, playtime, car rides to appointments, and when they are introduced to new people. Speak to your child as though they understand what you are saying, because many times they do, despite not having the verbal skills to engage. You can also consider taking baby sign language classes that can teach both you and your baby (older than 6 months) simple signs for commonly used words and needs. Experts have found that taking these classes accelerates verbal language development (Infante, 2024).

Chapter 10:

Strategies for Preschoolers (3–5 years)

Just Remember: The future is not some place you are going to, but one you are creating. The paths to it are not found but made. –John H. Schaar

Getting Off the Couch and Exploring the World

When your child joins the 3–5-year-old club, you may find it difficult to get them to sit down or stay in one place. Their curiosity has expanded from staring at people and objects to being hands-on and interacting with them. Learning occurs through creative, sensory stimulating play that allows them to use their eyes, ears, nose, mouth, and hands to understand how the world works. Children in this age group are allowed up to one hour of screen time daily. If you plan on exposing them to screens, break down this huge chunk of time into smaller intervals of 15–20 minutes, with technology breaks in between, to prevent your child from staring at their screens for too long. If possible, most of your child's time should be spent playing, whether it is outside or a designated play area indoors. At this age, you can give them instructions on how games or activities are carried out and they would be more than happy to play independently.

Making screen-free play fun will be your number one mission. If your child can find ways to entertain themselves and actually enjoy it, then they won't be thinking about their screens. Now and again, create opportunities for your child to participate in group games or activities. At first, let them get comfortable playing with you and their siblings. Teach them basic social skills that are essential to group play, like sharing, patience, and compromise. Once they have those basic skills down, expose them to different types of peer circles and social group activities where they get to play and socialize with other kids.

Older generations usually criticize the younger generations for becoming less engaged and intellectually curious when it comes to learning and maintaining relationships. While there are pros and cons to this argument, one of the reasons why the younger generations don't seem to "care" is because they live in the digital age where you don't need to put effort into developing skills to get what you want. They can type a prompt and get ChatGPT to solve their math sums, use emojis to convey emotions rather than express them using words, or replace their real friends with virtual ones who make them feel good all the time.

Your child, who's only 3–5 years old, doesn't have these problems yet. They are still at the tender age where their behaviors can be modified with loving but firm guidance. Too much exposure to technology during this stage of their life can prevent them from learning critical social, emotional, behavioral, and communication skills.

It's important for your child to not only be able to take care of their basic needs but to also understand how and where they fit into the world.

Ideas for Educational and Creative Activities That Do Not Involve Screens

During screen-free times, there are many ways that you can keep your child busy and stimulated. Below are some ideas that are both educational and creative.

Create an Experimental Space

When you have young children, you realize that making a mess is a sign of learning and creative problem-solving taking place. This doesn't mean that you want your child to make a mess in every room of the house. Create a space in your home where your child can engage in messy experimental activities such as painting, working with clay or play dough, or completing science projects. Make sure that all the materials they need are available so they don't need to leave the area. They can also leave their artistic masterpieces there to dry or to work on another time.

Second-Chance Play Box

When objects around the home have been broken or are no longer functional, think of placing them inside your child's second-chance play box before throwing them away. The second-chance play box is used whenever your child is engaging in imaginative play where they role-play real-life events and situations using costumes and props. The more diverse the materials inside the box are, the more creative your child needs to be to create real stories and scenarios around them. For example, with an old landline and prescription glasses (only the frame), your child can pretend to be several professionals they have learned about at school. They can also imitate how older family members speak on the phone or pretend to be processing a request given by someone on the other side of the line.

Build and Tear Down

One of the markers of intelligence is the ability to turn abstract ideas into tangible results and test assumptions to arrive at different conclusions (Chen & Li, 2014). A young child's favorite question to ask is: *Why?* This is because they want to understand the relationship between things. Instead of spoon-feeding your child answers and putting a stop to their curiosity, encourage them to seek the answers by building or tearing things apart. For example, if your child asks you what makes cars move, you can buy a toy car and get them to take it apart so they can see the different parts and learn about the function of each. If your child is curious about why cakes rise in the oven, bake two together—one with a leavening agent like baking soda and the other without. Let them spot and taste the difference.

Turn Ideas Into Designs

Young children are not short of ideas. They constantly daydream about ways they can make their lives or those of others richer and more fulfilling. What's fascinating about children between 3–5 years old is that they sincerely believe they can achieve their wildest dreams. To promote innovative thinking and goal-setting at this young age, encourage your child to put their dreams on paper and start working on them right away. Help them create a goal statement and 2–3 steps or tasks they need to complete to achieve their dream.

Note that many of their dreams may not be realistic or feasible but together, you can create a prototype that comes close to what they had imagined. For example, if your 4-year-old daughter dreams of turning her bedroom into "unicorn heaven" where she is surrounded by unicorns (fictional animals), draft a plan on how you can update her bedroom to add colors, fabrics, and accessories that come close to capturing her idea.

The Role of Parents in Helping Children Build Positive Peer Relationships

Young children don't know acceptable and unacceptable behaviors. They are taught by correcting their mistakes, role-playing common social scenarios, and offering age-appropriate explanations about why some behaviors are loved and others aren't. Social skills training therefore begins at home by setting rules and expectations for your child. Over time, these expectations become ingrained in their mind as "normal" ways of relating to others.

For example, if you don't want your child to get into the habit of requesting to watch TV when they arrive at someone else's house, set rules at home that manage how and when screens are accessed. You can also make screen-free games and activities the "normal" form of entertainment at home to help your child manage their expectations when they visit another household.

If you want your child to be social, friendly, and cooperative when they participate in group activities, use everyday home interactions as practice for how they should behave toward others. For example, to get your child accustomed to sharing their thoughts and feelings with others, make them feel comfortable expressing their views around the dinner table and during family bonding activities. Listen and validate your child's opinions to help them build confidence in speaking publicly.

If sharing and taking turns is an important skill you want them to learn, make it an expectation at home. With siblings, divide whatever you give them into equal portions. Instead of buying laptops for every child, buy one to share between them. If your child doesn't have siblings, create situations where they need to share with their pets, neighbors, or classmates. You can also teach an only child delayed gratification by not always giving them what they want immediately. They may need to wait for certain conditions to occur before their request is fulfilled.

You may also desire your child to speak a certain way with their peers or adults. Once again, use your home as the perfect training ground for communication skills. Role-play different scenarios where they may need to engage with different types of people like school teachers, doctors, or their extended family members. Step out from your parent role and into the roles of these people and imagine how you would want your child to address you. Correct their tone of voice, language, posture, gestures, and other cues that could be misinterpreted. Most importantly, explain why each type of person responds differently to their message depending on how it is delivered. For example, looking at the floor when speaking to your friend doesn't make a difference, but when speaking to a teacher, it can make them think you are not paying attention or interested in what they have to say.

There is a long list of social skills that 3- to 5-year-olds are capable of learning and practicing at their age. These include skills such as how to:

- cope with strong emotions

- listen to others without interrupting

- show empathy and compassion

- apologize after making a mistake

- solve social problems by coming up with win-win outcomes

Remember that these skills are not common sense for children. They need to be introduced as rules and expectations and reinforced continuously in a safe home environment. Praise your child for their efforts and progress, focusing on behaviors you love and approve of rather than criticizing them for behaviors you find worrisome. To make social skills training fun and motivating, consider creating a reward system around performing positive social behaviors.

As mentioned earlier in the chapter, incorporating group play and activities into your child's routine is important to teach them how to relate with other people. Fortunately, your child is at the age where they are discovering who they are and are open to exploring different social settings. By joining parent groups and communities, you can find other moms and dads who are looking for playmates for their young children. Your child may also enjoy the atmosphere of drama or dance clubs, gymnastic or martial arts classes, and other group sports or membership societies. The value of these group experiences is that your child learns to adjust their mindset, attitude, and behaviors based on their social surroundings and how they may be expected to show up.

Chapter 11:

Strategies for Elementary School Children (6–12 years)

The illiterate of the 21st century will not be those who cannot read and write, but those who cannot learn, unlearn, and relearn. —Alvin Toffler

Balancing Your Boundaries With Your Child's Technology Needs

The screen time guidelines offered by the American Academy of Pediatrics (2024) suggest allowing up to 1–1.5 hours of screen usage daily, and no more than 3 hours when your child has specific needs to carry out such as research or homework assignments. To your child, this may not feel like sufficient time to watch all of their programs, complete missions on their video games, and still stay updated on conversations happening in their friendship group chats. Left alone with their devices, they would spend most of the day online. However, this stage of your child's life is when executive functioning skills like critical thinking, planning, organizational skills, time management, and creative problem-solving become crucial.

Too much screen time is not only a distraction in your child's life but also delays their process of learning vital life skills. With that said, the solution is not to confiscate their devices or set rigid rules that prevent any amount of screen time. Rather, they need to be given access to technology to learn healthy ways of managing their usage and striking a balance between work and fun.

To positively influence your child's behaviors, try to empathize with their needs at this stage of their development. What could be important to your child right now? Most children won't mention education, even though, later in life, they will see how much of a vital role it played in shaping who they are. Instead, they will mention things like making friends, playing sports, or becoming a pro at gaming. Your duty as a parent is to help them balance *what they need to do* with *what they desire to do*.

If you are a parent who is completely against screens, try to be more open and flexible to accommodate your child's technology needs. You don't need to share the same interests as them to acknowledge why they matter. Here are some ways that you can meet your child in the middle and balance your boundaries with their technology needs.

Determine the What, When, Where, and How

You won't be with your child 24/7 when they are at home. In your absence, they need to understand your expectations around screen usage and what they can or cannot do.

Set up a family meeting with your child present and discuss the 3-Ws-and-H of technology:

1. What devices, apps, websites, and content is your child allowed to access?

2. When during the weekdays and weekends is your child allowed to use technology?

3. Where around the house are devices allowed or banned?

4. How should your child use their devices or engage with various media content or internet users?

These questions are normally covered in the family media plan, so if you haven't created one yet, it's recommended that you do so (refer to Part 5 for the template). Knowing the 3-Ws-and-H of technology enables your child to practice self-control and take ownership of their screen habits, two very critical skills that can promote a strong and stable identity.

Work First, Play Later

Play is an essential component of a healthy childhood. However, as children get older, the role of play changes. For example, for kids under five years old, play is the best form of learning and skills development. Children older than five still need time for play to improve social-emotional skills, but they learn best by observing, exploring, listening, asking questions, and experimenting. In other words, through taking actions (and learning from their actions), your child strengthens their abilities. Therefore, they cannot run away from doing "hard things" because, through effort, not perfection, they acquire new skills and knowledge. The "work first, play later" concept is supposed to remind your child of which tasks take priority. If they are presented with an option to watch a YouTube video or complete a house chore, the one that requires work (i.e., the house chore) must be done first. You can also remind your child of this concept by rewarding their work with screen time. For example, if your child has completed their schoolwork, packed their school bag, and taken the dog for a walk, with a few hours remaining before dinner (no screen time rewards should be given an hour before bedtime), they can earn screen time.

Manage Your Expectations Around Technology

Technology comes with advantages and disadvantages, depending on how you integrate it into your home life. When creating screen limits and boundaries, don't fall into the temptation of only seeing the bad side of technology and downplaying the good. Expose your child to gadgets that you can afford to bring inside the home and teach them how to practice moderation.

Explore ways that you can use technology to bridge the generation gap between you and your child while promoting healthy habits. For instance, you can use a GPS to find a route taking you to the nearby shops or restaurants. During nature walks, you can encourage your child to take pictures of the interesting things they see.

Creating a Healthy Homework Routine

Earlier in Chapter 7, we discussed the value of structured routines in helping to minimize screen usage and promote productive habits throughout the day. We mentioned how routines can be themed and focused on reinforcing daily tasks such as completing homework. For many elementary children, homework is an undesirable task that's either left to the last minute or conveniently lost around the house.

Some children might rush through their homework and make careless mistakes, all so that they can extend their screen time. Even though homework is a compulsory task, getting your child to look forward to their homework routine can improve their attitude and approach toward school work. Instead of thinking of homework as a task to quickly check off their list, whether they understand the concepts or not, they can find pleasure in their structured, supportive, and enjoyable homework routine. Below are some strategies that you can implement to create a healthy homework routine.

Meet With the Teacher

Find out from your child's teacher how much homework they receive each day (and from which subjects). They can also give you a general guideline on how much time your child should be spending on homework for each grade. During the meeting, find out about your child's classroom performance and behaviors to assess the skills they need to practice more at home. If you have any concerns about your child's attitude toward at-home learning, raise them with their teacher and ask for suggestions on how to motivate them. If possible, meet with your child's teacher each semester to review your child's progress.

Draft a Homework Agreement With Your Child

Once you have an idea of your child's homework needs, sit them down and provide age-appropriate feedback. Let them know the areas where they are excelling and where they need to make more effort. Hear from them to understand what type of support they need. For example, do they need help practicing reading, writing, or counting? Or do they often feel tired when doing homework and need something to keep them energized and entertained?

On a piece of paper, draw up a homework agreement explaining how homework will be carried out. Let your child take the lead in suggesting rules and expectations since this will increase their motivation. Guide them when it comes to establishing structure, such as choosing the time of day, duration, and workstation. Encourage fun elements like playing soft music, having dance or snack breaks, and earning reward points for every successful homework session (which can be exchanged at the end of the month for a tangible prize).

Make Homework a Bonding Experience

Elementary-aged children are capable of doing homework with minimal supervision. However, this doesn't mean that they should. If you are a stay-at-home parent or return from work just before homework time, consider sitting in on your child's homework sessions. You don't necessarily have to be over their shoulder, helping out with each question. You could be within walking distance, doing a quiet task like ironing or folding laundry.

Having someone with them in the room can help them stay focused on their tasks for longer. They also won't have the fear of missing out (FOMO) from being alone while the rest of the family is together. At the start of each homework session, ask your child to outline the objectives they would like to achieve by the end. When the session ends, have them report on whether they were able to achieve those objectives or not, and why. Periodically, during each session, ask if they are okay and need some help or would like to take a break.

Encouraging Hobbies

When it's time to put the books away and have fun, promote recreational activities that don't involve watching screens. This may not always be possible with your child at this age because they have already formed interests and preferences. For instance, if your child likes to spend their free time watching other people play games on live stream (a hobby that many young people enjoy), you may find it difficult to convince them to kick a ball outside or make an effort to socialize with their friends in real life. Even by reducing their screen time, they may not want to leave the house or engage in screen-free activities.

Furthermore, the older children get, the less open they are to being told what to do. Indeed, enrolling in a team sport or learning a musical instrument would offer so many benefits to your child, but only if that was their idea, not yours. Therefore, as much as you want your child to have more offline experiences, they have to buy into this vision and feel motivated to change their lifestyle habits.

Guiding your child toward discovering their hobbies is perhaps the best way to distract them from screens and be grounded in the present moment. Hobbies are recreational activities that your child is curious or passionate about. Most times, they are connected to your child's strengths and talents, so learning what your child is naturally good at can help you identify potential hobbies. Early exposure to diverse ideas, beliefs, and experiences gives your child the chance to imagine what goals they can achieve. Their hobbies could be based on memorable family outings, celebrations, or personal achievements they have had in the past. Your child could also be fascinated by your interests or occupation and end up dreaming of walking in your footsteps.

Encouraging your child to pursue their hobbies isn't about forcing them to do as many activities as you can fit into their schedule, hoping they fall in love with a few of them. Allow your child to set the pace with their level of curiosity. Simply ask questions and create opportunities where they can attend the classes or events they are curious about. If they don't show any interest past the first session, don't push them to attend the second one. Shift your focus to whatever new experience they are curious about and show enthusiasm about arranging a physical class or visit.

Eventually, your child will find hobbies that they cannot stop talking about. They may even beg to attend more sessions or develop their skills in that particular craft or sport. This is the perfect moment to explain the tradeoffs they need to make to fit their hobbies into their daily schedule. For example, if they enjoy swimming, they will need to make time to attend training sessions and competitions. As a result, the free time available on weekdays and weekends will be reduced. Added to this, their swimming instructor may expect them to make some lifestyle changes to improve their athletic abilities such as eating less junk food and going to bed at a certain time.

If your child can willingly accept these tradeoffs and frame them in a positive way, you will witness their lifestyle positively transforming and screens becoming a less important feature. The bonus is that showing commitment to anything, including school work and hobbies, strengthens your child's character and shapes them into a disciplined and self-motivated individual.

Chapter 12:

Strategies for Teenagers (13–18 years)

As we say in technology: garbage in, garbage out. We know we're products of the food we eat. Why wouldn't we also be products of the information we consume? –Clay A. Johnson

Social Challenges Caused By Too Much Screen Time

Adolescence is a transitional stage where your son or daughter goes from being classified as a child to an adult. The skills and knowledge they learn during this stage are designed to provide a stable foundation, helping them thrive as young adults. As with any other growth phase, a lot of changes happen to your child on a physical, cognitive, and emotional level. Don't be surprised if they aren't the same agreeable and cheerful child they were years ago—they are in the process of forming a mature identity and may outgrow their childlike traits, interests, and beliefs. Nevertheless, your child is not an adult yet and needs plenty of guidance and mentorship to build a healthy and meaningful life. They may not like to hear it being said, but the truth is that there is a lot they still don't know and need to be coached on. One crucial aspect of your child's life where they need support is building and nurturing relationships. Without a strong support network, your child may struggle to find stability in their personal and professional lives.

Our society is made up of people playing different roles to survive and succeed. These roles, although demanding, provide a sense of belonging and achievement. When your child is confused about the roles they need to play and how they can collaborate with others to achieve common goals, they may feel anxious about making social connections and even afraid to interact with people.

Many electronic devices are built in such a way that you don't need to be seen by others. While video chats and conference calls exist, the majority of online communication happens over images, premade videos, text messaging, listening to audio recordings, and of course, reacting with emojis or leaving a "like." Teens who are dependent on technology simply don't get enough human contact and real-life conversations. They may be experts at navigating their online communities, such as growing their following and making virtual friends. However, the skills used to form digital connections aren't the same social skills used to build lasting physical relationships.

The most disturbing social challenge that tech-dependent teens are experiencing is they don't feel prepared for their real-world social roles. Due to the time spent developing their digital identities, they have missed out on discovering who they are offline, what their strengths and weaknesses are, and what tangible contribution they see themselves making in the world. They may appear clueless when asked about future employment, financial planning, family planning, and other parts of their life that require careful thought. Some may develop social anxiety and struggle to relate to people who are not part of their digital community (e.g., non-gamers) because all of the knowledge they have spent years researching and gathering is specifically related to their obsession with gaming.

The allure of the internet, especially social media, is how easy it is for your child to find like-minded people who embrace the same views, beliefs, and lifestyle choices as they do. But this can also be dangerous because, in the real world, your child will face different kinds of social situations and meet a diverse group of people, who may not have the same qualities, humor, outlook, and behaviors as them. Without social skills and emotional intelligence, they may freeze, not knowing what others expect from them.

Another challenge tech-dependent teens may face is being open and cooperative in group settings. Excessive screen time leads to social isolation, which limits group bonding experiences. Most of the time, your child may be alone in their bedroom, scrolling through their phone or surfing the net. While many online communities support group discussions by sharing thoughts and commenting on other people's posts, these discussions are superficial, unnatural, and may present a false feeling of connection.

For example, it's normal to read an interesting caption on social media and leave a comment to continue the dialogue with the person who published it. But in real life, you wouldn't walk over to a stranger and share your thoughts, would you? Even if you found their actions thought-provoking, there are social codes that we live by that prevent you from having free discussions with people you don't know, as though you had known them for years. In the same way, the online communities that your child is a part of do not equip them with the social-emotional skills they need to build real friends and make a contribution to real communities because digital social standards are different from real-world social standards.

Basic Social Skills to Teach Your Teen at Home

It's worth emphasizing that social challenges won't be the only challenges your child faces when they go through adolescence. However, this specific challenge is one of the common ones related to screen dependency and addiction, and with your early intervention, you can positively turn things around for your child.

Your safe and predictable home environment is the best place to practice basic social skills with your teen. They are familiar with you and other family members and may feel less anxious stepping out of their comfort zone. Before attempting any social skills training, rule out possible mental health or learning disabilities that could be affecting your child's sociability. Arrange a doctor's visit to assess their overall well-being and see whether there could be more to their social behaviors, such as an anxiety disorder or autism spectrum disorder (ASD).

Moreover, take a day or two to reflect on your intentions for teaching your child social skills. Consider what you hope they can gain from developing their skills. While it's good to motivate your child to be more open to meeting people and building relationships, they may still have social preferences such as enjoying solitude more than group activities. Respect their social preferences by giving them the tools to navigate different social interactions without forcing them to do anything they may be uncomfortable with.

Your approach matters when empowering your teen with social skills. The moment they feel judged, undermined, or controlled, they may react defensively and show little to no interest in this initiative.

Manage your expectations when it comes to setting expectations for your child. For example, a socially awkward teenager won't become a social butterfly overnight (and may not even desire to be one). However, with ongoing practice, they can learn how to start conversations, show curiosity in others, or contribute ideas or opinions in group settings. This would still be an achievement.

It's also crucial to express in words and actions that you accept your child for who they are. Having strong social skills can open doors for them later in life; however, they are still lovable and worthy as they are. The world may treat them differently with versus without proper social skills, but your love for them is unchanging.

Below are suggestions for basic social skills that you can introduce your child to at home. For more advanced skills, consider seeking the services of a psychologist or counselor.

Making Small Talk

We have been taught to avoid small talk because of how improvised the conversations are. Some may even associate small talk with insincerity or "trying too hard." The truth is that all great conversations start small, with an idea thrown on the table. It doesn't have to be an extravagant idea; just one that can be unpacked and probed further.

The difference between a "good small talker" and a "bad small talker" is how well they listen. When you are focused on what someone is saying, you can find multiple ways to expand on their idea. Think of how we create mind maps when brainstorming: 10 ideas can all be traced back to one simple main idea. Without effective listening, you make assumptions about where the conversation is leading and thus choose not to engage, or do so half-heartedly.

Knowing how to have small talk will help your child introduce themselves in new environments, get to know new acquaintances, and help others know a little more about them. Engaging in small talk can also make them appear friendly, welcoming, intelligent, and confident.

Use role-play to reenact scenarios where your child may need to engage in small talk, such as waiting in a queue, speaking to a potential boss in an interview, meeting new friends, and so on. Their task is to listen attentively and collect information so they can respond with a question or share a related story. You can also switch roles and show your child how to initiate small talk and subtle nonverbal cues to be mindful of, like eye contact, body posture, and facial expressions.

Reading Social Cues

Social cues are clues that let you know what someone else is thinking without them having to tell you. For example, yawning while someone is talking is a sign of boredom. Crossing arms or legs when facing someone is a sign of defensiveness. Reading social cues is a valuable skill for your child to learn because it strengthens their social awareness, self-awareness, and ability to show empathy for others. In social settings, they can interpret positive and negative feedback from others by recognizing the cues and changing their behavior accordingly.

There are different types of social cues that you can teach your child, such as body language, facial expressions, tone of voice, and personal space. Body language refers to the way someone moves their body. Movements that make the body small and caved in, like droopy shoulders, lowered head, crossed arms, or turning away from people signal disinterest, withdrawal, or defensiveness. Movements that make the body bigger, like wide eyes, open arms, handshakes, smiling, standing and sitting straight, nodding, and leaning toward people signal warmth, trust, and interest. Facial expressions are used to help communicate how we're feeling. Little to no expression on the face can be seen as a sign of disinterest or boredom. In different social settings, more or less expression is required.

However, generally, something as simple as raising your eyebrows when someone mentions an interesting fact or smiling when someone tells a joke or speaks about something they are passionate about can go a long way in making them feel validated.

The tone of voice is another social cue to be careful of. Changing your tone of voice from low to high or slow to fast can signal different moods and attitudes.

Personal space between you and others reveals the degree of emotional closeness you share. In professional settings, particularly, it's important to respect personal space and not get too close to others without standing or sitting too far, which gives off the message that you want to be left alone.

Professional Writing

Learning how to write formal emails and messages is another important social skill to teach your child. It enables them to assess the audience they are writing to and choose the most fitting language to convey their ideas. How the receiver interprets the message is more important than the intention behind it.

This is because, on paper or over email exchanges, there aren't any nonverbal cues to help analyze what is being said. Therefore, being clear and direct while also being mindful of word choice and phrasing can be the difference between mistakenly offending someone and making them feel appreciated.

Managing Social Media Use

A common meeting place for teens on the internet is social media. This is where they get to share and engage with content and connect with users who share similar interests. A 2022 survey found that 35% of children between 13–17 visited at least one out of five main social media platforms (i.e., YouTube, Meta, Instagram, TikTok, and Snapchat), several times during the day (Mayo Clinic Staff, 2024).

From the age of 13, your child can open social media accounts on various platforms. This could be something they are looking forward to about becoming a teenager. Social media isn't necessarily bad for your child, however, as the saying goes, too much of anything is never healthy. Instead of restricting your child from using social media, teach them healthy ways to manage their social media use. By doing this, you are showing them how to practice self-control and make wise decisions concerning their well-being.

When it comes to managing social media use, have an open discussion about when, where, and how long your child can be on social media each day. Since they are old enough to create their own schedules, allow them to take the lead and suggest appropriate times, places, and durations for being on social media. You can negotiate different rules for weekdays, weekends, special occasions, and school holidays.

Another crucial conversation to have with your child is what social media can and cannot be used for. Many young people share their lives on their social media pages, revealing personal information, painful stories from their past, and sexual photos or intimate moments with their partners. Remind your child that everything they post, comment on, or engage with leaves a digital footprint, which can negatively impact their reputation a few years down the line when they are looking for employment or desire to enter a serious relationship.

Indeed, social media promotes being yourself, however, since it's still a public network, self-awareness and dignified behaviors must be shown. A rule of thumb is to ask yourself: *If my social media post was blown up on a billboard for everyone to see, would it be a good reflection of who I am?*

Here are a few examples of what social media should and shouldn't be used for. Go through these examples with your child and let them share their opinions.

Social media should be used for

- being creative

- joining interest-based groups

- staying updated on trends

- showing support for worthy causes

- sharing aspects of your life that could inspire others

- learning useful hacks, skills, and advice from experts

- making friends with other teens locally and internationally

Social media should not be used for

- bullying others

- venting your frustrations or processing grief

- spreading rumors or leaving hurtful comments

- substituting real friendships and communities

- entertaining yourself when you are bored or cannot sleep

- distracting yourself from studying or other important tasks

Many teens won't feel enthusiastic about having their social media accounts monitored by their parents. To get around this, you can make an agreement with your child to conduct a review and "cleanup" of their social media accounts once every quarter. For a few days, they can give you access to their accounts so you can observe what they are posting, how they are engaging with others, who they are communicating with, what pages or groups they are following, and so on. This could be followed by a heart-to-heart feedback session and cleanup (if necessary).

Present your concerns, identifying posts or interactions that you found worrying, and explain why. Ask your child to remove the posts, block the user, unfollow the page, or whatever measures they need to put in place to stay safe.

Part 5:

Interactive Activities and

Worksheets

Chapter 13:

Screen-Free Activity Ideas

Every social association that is not face-to-face is injurious to your health.
—Nassim Nicholas Taleb

Screen-Free Activities for Toddlers (0–2 years)

The following list presents screen-free activities suitable for children between 0–2 years.

Singing to Nursery Rhymes

Entertain your toddler by singing for them. Use animated facial expressions and body movements to keep them captivated. Remember to sing at a slow pace and articulate your words to increase vocabulary recognition.

Playing With Playdough

Place a ball of playdough on a tray that your child can play with. Make a few shapes or figures to demonstrate what they can do with it.

This simple activity strengthens their fine motor skills and hand-eye coordination. Since little ones may be tempted to put play dough in their mouth, make one using edible ingredients.

Read Picture Books

Introduce your child to new sounds and words by reading picture books. Change your voice and pitch to create a stimulating auditory experience. While reading, point to words or images on the page to help your toddler connect what they hear and see.

Sensory Board

Create a sensory board with safe materials sourced around the house, such as pieces of fabric, keys, zippers, jewelry, and so on.

Combine different colors, textures, and shapes to give your child hours' worth of stimulation. Make sure that the materials are securely glued or attached to the board so that your child cannot pull them off.

Screen-Free Activities for Preschoolers (3–5 years)

The following list presents screen-free activities suitable for children between 3–5 years.

Coloring

Buy coloring books or print out coloring pages online that your child can use. Present them with pictures of objectives, animals, or things they are fascinated by. For example, if your child is fascinated by dinosaurs, search for a dinosaur-themed coloring book.

Puppet-Making

At 3–5 years, your child is learning new words and phrases at an accelerated speed. To encourage them to talk, help them make puppets using socks and art materials. Ask them to give their puppet a name and personality traits. You can create a puppet too and role-play different social scenarios together.

Baking

Baking is a fun and tasty way to teach your child how to remember sequences of steps and follow instructions. Furthermore, the process of turning ingredients into baked goods can stimulate your child's imagination, helping them to become a creative thinker.

Scavenger Hunts

When your child is bored but has a lot of energy, set up a scavenger hunt around the house or outside. Hide themed objectives in different places and give your child clues to help find them.

This activity tests their memory, attention, problem-solving, vocabulary recognition, and resilience.

Screen-Free Activities for Elementary School Children (6–12 years)

The following list presents screen-free activities suitable for children between 6–12 years.

Board Games

If your child enjoys the adventure and competition of computer games, introduce them to various board games that range from simple to challenging.

Go for games that have an educational component, such as teaching numeracy, wordplay, memorization, and life skills. Board games that require groups are perfect for family bonding time.

Arts and Crafts

To keep your child busy and mentally stimulated, encourage them to get creative. Arts and crafts activities range from doodling on a page to creating a science experiment. You can also use arts and crafts to teach your child the importance of recycling and upcycling, and of thinking innovatively.

Visit Local Attractions

Make going outside fun by touring local attractions such as art galleries, zoos, aquariums, and museums with your child. Not only are these types of outings educational, but they also expose your child to unique social settings where they can practice social skills like listening, asking questions, and making small talk.

Martial Arts

Martial arts is more than just a sport. It teaches your child self-defense skills, self-discipline, and respect for themselves and others. Over time, martial arts can boost your child's confidence, reduce rebellious behaviors, and promote healthy coping strategies.

Screen-Free Activities for Teenagers (13–18 years)

The following list presents screen-free activities suitable for children between 13–18 years.

DJing

For many teens, music is a therapeutic tool that helps them unwind and provides an escape from the real world. If you notice that your child enjoys music, encourage them to learn the art of mixing songs, producing beats, and creating their own music.

If possible, get your child a physical DJ set instead of downloading DJ software. Motivate them to make DJing social by inviting their friends to listening parties.

Outdoor Adventure Sports

Older children may not be excited to go outside unless there is a big enough incentive. Outdoor adventure sports are the perfect incentive. These range from boot camps, extreme obstacle courses, mountain biking, paintballing, and quad biking. These sports produce the same (and even more) adrenaline than video games.

Volunteering

Socializing can be daunting for teens. To give them a head start, consider enrolling them in an ongoing volunteer program. They can choose a cause close to their heart, such as caring for animals or the environment. Being involved in the program offers them an opportunity to network with people of different ages, races, and cultural backgrounds, and learn valuable life skills.

Cooking

Cooking is a creative and therapeutic activity that some teens may enjoy. They will improve their culinary skills while finding positive ways to express themselves. To motivate your child to cook, buy them cookbooks, kitchen utensils, and gadgets, and give positive feedback when they present their meals.

Chapter 14:

Sample Schedules

Technology is just a tool. In terms of getting the kids working together and motivating them, the teacher is the most important. –Bill Gates

Daily Schedule With Limited Screen Time

The following daily schedule integrates appropriate amounts of screen time into your child's daily routine. Feel free to modify this schedule according to the screen guidelines outlined for your child's age (refer to Chapter 1):

- **7:30 a.m.:** Wake up and breakfast (screen-free)

- **8:00 a.m.:** Schoolwork or educational activities

- **10:00 a.m.:** Outdoor play or physical activity

- **11:00 a.m.:** Screen time (1 hour, including educational apps or games)

- **12:00 p.m.:** Lunch (screen-free)

- **1:00 p.m.:** Nap or quiet time

- **2:00 p.m.:** Homework or reading

- **3:00 p.m.:** Creative activities (arts and crafts, building)

- **3:30 p.m.:** Screen time (30 minutes, educational or recreational)

- **5:00 p.m.:** Dinner (screen-free)

- **6:00 p.m.:** Family activities (board games, cooking together)

- **7:00 p.m.:** Relaxation or winding down (story time, puzzle)

- **8:00 p.m.:** Bedtime routine (screen-free)

Screen Time Reward Schedule

The following schedule integrates screen time into your child's daily routine; however, uses screen time as an earned privilege for completing tasks. The schedule may change day-by-day depending on your child's motivation and consistency. Feel free to modify this schedule to reflect your child's everyday routine:

- **8:00 a.m.:** Morning routine (screen-free)

- **9:00 a.m.:** Schoolwork or chores (earn 30 minutes of screen time for completion)

- **12:00 p.m.:** Lunch (screen-free)

- **1:00 p.m.:** Creative activities or outdoor play

- **2:00 p.m.:** Screen time (30 minutes as a reward for completing morning tasks)

- **3:00 p.m.:** Homework or additional chores (earn 30 minutes of screen time)

- **5:00 p.m.:** Family time or physical activity

- **6:00 p.m.:** Screen time (30 minutes as a reward for completing afternoon tasks)

- **7:00 p.m.:** Dinner (screen-free)

- **8:00 p.m.:** Relaxation or family activity (screen-free)

- **8:30 p.m.:** Bedtime routine

Media Viewing and Device Schedules

The following schedules focus on creating more structure around the media content and electronic devices your child is allowed to view or access during screen time, throughout the week. You can modify the schedules to include the forms of media and devices your child uses.

Day	Time	TV show name	Channel	PG
Monday	7:30 p.m.	The Big Bang Theory	CBS	PG 14
	8:00 p.m.	Stranger Things	Netflix	PG 14

	Monday	**Tuesday**	**Wednesday**	**Thursday**	**Friday**
TV					
Start time:					
Finish time:					
Total time:					
Smartphone					
Start time:					
Finish time:					
Total time:					
Computer					

Day	Time	TV show name		Channel	PG
Start time:					
Finish time:					
Total time:					
Screen use daily total:					
Earned screen time:					
Did you adhere to the daily allowance?					

Chapter 15:

Worksheets

While technology is important, it's what we do with it that truly matters. —
Muhammad Yunus

Introduction to Worksheets

The following worksheets provide a range of tools to manage
your child's screen time, establish rules and boundaries, and
monitor the impact of technology on their well-being.

You are welcome to modify these worksheets according to your
family's needs and schedules.

Screen Time Log

Date	Devices used	Screen activity	Duration of screen time	Mood and behavior observations
Monday	tablet	educational programming	30 minutes	focused and engaged
Tuesday				
Wednesday				
Thursday				
Friday				
Saturday				
Sunday				

Screen Time Checklist

Before using screens, did you...	Mon	Tues	Wed	Thurs	Fri	Sat	Sun
make your bed?							
eat breakfast?							
complete your chores?							
complete homework?							
take a nap?							
play with your siblings?							
spend time with your family?							
go outside?							
read something?							

Screen Time Reduction Goal Sheet

	Current average screen time	Desired reduction goal	Daily or weekly plan to achieve the goal	Progress report
TV				
Smartphone				
Computer				
Video games				
Tablet				

Behavior Observation Sheet

Date	Location	Activity	What happened right before?	Troubling behavior	What happened right after?	Comments
15th July	Afternoon, at home	Playing computer games	Matthew was asked to turn off his computer and walk the dog.	yelling, complaining, and refusing to log out	Screen rewards have been paused for the next 2 days.	–

Family Media Plan Template

Family Values

As the [Last Name] family, our mission statement is to

_____

_____

_____

_____

_____

_____

_____

_____

_____

_____

_____

_____

To achieve this mission, we need to implement a family media plan that creates a healthy balance between bonding time, personal enrichment time, and screen time.

Screen Limits

Each family member (including adults) must adhere to their specific screen limits, depending on their age. In our home, we will allow up to:

[Family member 1]:

_____ minutes/hours per day of screen time.

[Family member 2]:

_____ minutes/hours per day of screen time.

[Family member 3]:

_____ minutes/hours per day of screen time.

[Family member 4]:

_____ minutes/hours per day of screen time.

[Family member 5]:

_____ minutes/hours per day of screen time.

Screen Curfews

Every family member (including adults) with a smartphone has a "device curfew."

At that specific time, all phones need to be charged overnight in a designated charging station.

Charging station area: _____

[Family member 1]:

_____ curfew time.

[Family member 2]:

_____ curfew time.

[Family member 3]:

_____ curfew time.

[Family member 4]:

_____ curfew time.

[Family member 5]:

_____ curfew time.

Screen-Free Zones

There are certain areas around our home where technology is not allowed. These areas include:

1. _____

2. _____

3. _____

4. _____

5. _____

Technology Rules

To ensure our safety and privacy while using technology, take note of the following rules:

1. Passwords:

_____

_____

_____

2. Personal information:

_____

_____

_____

_____

3. Parent monitoring:

_____

_____

_____

_____

4. Content sharing:

_____

_____

_____

_____

5. Online friends and communities:

_____

_____

_____

_____

6. Inappropriate online behaviors:

_____

_____

_____

_____

7. Texting etiquette:

_____

_____

_____

_____

_____

8. Balancing online and offline activities:

_____

_____

_____

_____

_____

9. Screen rewards and bonus time:

_____

_____

_____

_____

_____

10. Social media reviews and clean-ups:

_____

_____

_____

_____

_____

Ongoing Tech Talks

There will be times when we make mistakes and forget to follow our family media plan closely.

To keep us motivated, we will meet regularly to have conversations about our screen needs and concerns.

In our home, we commit to having tech talks every

_____

Signatures

This family media plan will be reviewed by our family every 6 months.

[Family member 1

name and signature]:_____

[Family member 2

name and signature]:_____

[Family member 3

name and signature]:_____

[Family member 4

name and signature]:_____

[Family member 5

name and signature]:_____

Conclusion

Technological society has succeeded in multiplying the opportunities for pleasure, but it has great difficulty in generating joy. —Pope Paul VI

The Path Forward

Technology is an ever-evolving component of modern society. The appeal of saving costs and time by automating tasks and digitizing entertainment has made it harder to resist integrating technology into your home. While the days of living tech-free may be behind you, that doesn't mean that your devices need to rule your home and family life. The purpose of this book was to explore the challenges that your child faces when they become dependent or addicted to screens and provide age-related strategies to prevent overexposure. As a parent, you are responsible for introducing your child to electronic devices and teaching them how to use them in moderation. For example, you get to decide whether watching TV is an entitlement or a privilege. Moreover, you determine the do's and don'ts of device usage. Indeed, your child may have access to multiple devices at home, but there can be screen limits enforced on each device, specifically times during the day, or zones at home where those devices aren't allowed.

You can also go a step further and design a family media plan that outlines the acceptable relationship each family member should strive to achieve with technology—including parents.

Without these protective measures, you can unintentionally cause your child to value online experiences more than they do offline, skill-enhancing experiences.

Moving forward, continue to educate yourself on the changing nature of technology and the latest devices that children are engaging. Have open conversations about technology with your child to learn more about their interests, favorite tech tools, and the online spaces they frequently visit. Let your curiosity be driven by seeking to keep them safe, offer support on how to balance their digital world with the real world, and develop the necessary skills to thrive in both.

If you are concerned about your child's screen use or the cognitive, social, and behavioral symptoms of excessive screen time they may be struggling with, consider seeking professional help from a licensed child therapist who can offer expert tools and guidance. Use this as an opportunity to also reflect on your parenting approach and ways that you may have given your child too much freedom on how and when they can use technology. Remember, your child learns their behaviors by watching your actions.

Lead by example by building healthy screen habits that promote spending more time playing, cuddling, laughing, and bonding with your family than working behind a laptop or smartphone. Ultimately, it's never too late to rescue your child from screen addiction and get them back to the bubbly, confident, and creative person they were. Make the effort to control the influence of technology in your home before it starts to control your family!

About the Author

Richard Bass is a well-established author with extensive knowledge and background on children's disabilities. Richard has also experienced first-hand many children and teens who deal with depression and anxiety. He enjoys researching techniques and ideas to better serve students, as well as guiding parents on how to understand and lead their children to success. Richard wants to share his experience, research, and practices through his writing, as it has proven successful for many parents and students.

Richard feels there is a need for parents and others around the child to fully understand the disability or the mental health of the child. He hopes that with his writing people will be more understanding of children going through these issues.

Richard Bass has been in education for over a decade and holds a bachelor's and master's degree in education as well as several certifications including Special Education K-12, and Educational Administration.

Whenever Richard is not working, reading, or writing he likes to travel with his family to learn about different cultures as well as get ideas from all around about the upbringing of children especially those with disabilities. Richard also researches and learns about different educational systems around the world.

Richard participates in several online groups where parents, educators, doctors, and psychologist share their success with children with disabilities. Richard is in the process of growing a Facebook group where further discussion about his books and techniques could take place. Apart from online groups, he has also attended trainings regarding the upbringing of students with disabilities and has also led trainings in this area.

A Message from the Author

If you enjoyed the book and are interested on further updates or just a place to share your thoughts with other readers or myself, please join my Facebook group by scanning below!

If you would be interested on receiving a FREE Planner for kids PDF version, by signing up you will also receive exclusive notifications to when new content is released and will be able to receive it at a promotional price. Scan below to sign up!

Scan below to check out my content on You Tube and learn more about Neurodiversity!

References

Ackerman, C. (2018, June 7). *What is self-concept theory? A psychologist explains.* Positive Psychology. https://positivepsychology.com/self-concept/

Adair, C. (2022, June 19). *Fifty best screen-free activities by age.* Game Quitters. https://gamequitters.com/best-screen-free-activities-by-age/

Addicted to technology? Discover the telltale signs of a tech addiction and 7 healthy ways to curb your digital habit. (2019, August 5). Inspiring Leadership Now. https://www.inspiringleadershipnow.com/how-to-overcome-tech-addiction/

Agarwal, A. (2024, July 16). *Importance of parental involvement in screen time for kids.* LinkedIn. https://www.linkedin.com/pulse/importance-parental-involvement-screen-time-kids-ashutosh-agarwal-mp76c/

Aggarwal, N. (2024, July 29). *The benefits of talking to baby in utero.* The Bump. https://www.thebump.com/a/talking-to-baby-in-utero

The American Academy of Child & Adolescent Psychiatry. (2024, May). *Screen time and children.* https://www.aacap.org/AACAP/Families_and_Youth/Facts_for_Families/FFF-Guide/Children-And-Watching-TV-054.aspx

American Academy of Pediatrics. (2021, July 26). *Social development in preschoolers*. Healthy Children. https://www.healthychildren.org/English/ages-stages/preschool/Pages/Social-Development-in-Preschoolers.aspx

American Psychological Association. (2008). *What parents should know about treatment of behavioral and emotional disorders in preschool children*. American Psychological Association. https://www.apa.org/topics/children/treatment-behavioral-emotional-disorders-preschoolers

Aubusson, L. (2021, June 16). *Parents believed son had 'severe ADHD' until mum cut TV shows and he completely changed*. Kid Spot. https://www.kidspot.com.au/news/my-sons-symptoms-of-adhd-disappeared-with-a-tv-detox/news-story/3935efb8891be2642cba97b7adbf685d

Ben-Joseph, E. P. (2022, August). *Monitoring your child's media use (for parents)*. KidsHealth. https://kidshealth.org/en/parents/monitor-media.html

Berthold, J. (2022, July 26). *Elevated tween screen time linked to disruptive behavior disorders*. University of California San Francisco. https://www.ucsf.edu/news/2022/07/423256/elevated-tween-screen-time-linked-disruptive-behavior-disorders

Beurkens, N. (2020, July 21). *How does technology affect children's social development?* Qustodio. https://www.qustodio.com/en/blog/technology-child-social-development/

Beurkens, N. (2023, April 19). *Does technology affect children's focus?* Qustodio. https://www.qustodio.com/en/blog/does-technology-affect-childrens-focus/

Bowyer, C. (2024, January 12). *What is digital identity? | Your guide to digital identity.* Onfido. https://onfido.com/blog/digital-identity/

Bradley Ruder, D. (2019, June 19). *Screen time and the brain.* Harvard Medical School. https://hms.harvard.edu/news/screen-time-brain

Brown, D. (2000). *A quote from Dan Brown.* Goodreads. https://www.goodreads.com/quotes/485921-even-the-technology-that-promises-to-unite-us-divides-us

Chen, M. L. (2023, September 7). *Here's how screen time is scaling sleep deprivation in teens.* World Economic Forum. https://www.weforum.org/agenda/2023/09/screen-time-affecting-sleep-mental-health/

Chen, Y., & Li, L. (2014). *Advances in intelligent vehicles.* Academic Press.

Cheriyedath, S. (2024, February 21). *How much physical activity do children need?* News-Medical. https://www.news-medical.net/health/How-Much-Physical-Activity-Do-Children-Need.aspx

Cherry, K. (2022, December 23). *Permissive parenting characteristics and effects.* Verywell Mind. https://www.verywellmind.com/what-is-permissive-parenting-2794957

Choukas-Bradley, S. (2022, April 17). How to talk with your kids about social media. *Psychology Today.* https://www.psychologytoday.com/za/blog/psychology-adolescence/202204/how-talk-your-kids-about-social-media

Clicks that build self-esteem. How technologies affect confidence. (2023, October 1). Safer Kids Online. https://saferkidsonline.eset.com/sg/article/clicks-that-build-self-esteem-how-technologies-affect-confidence

Cooper, J. A. (n.d.). *Screens and your sleep: The impact of nighttime use.* Sutter Health. https://www.sutterhealth.org/health/sleep/screens-and-your-sleep-the-impact-of-nighttime-use

Coping strategies for teen socializing. (2023, November 17). Newport Academy. https://www.newportacademy.com/resources/empowering-teens/teens-and-socializing/

Cottrell, S. (2020, January 2). *A year-by-year guide to the different generations and their personalities.* Parents. https://www.parents.com/parenting/better-parenting/style/generation-names-and-years-a-cheat-sheet-for-parents/

Create good homework habits with this 3-step plan. (2022, July 5). Scholastic. https://www.scholastic.com/parents/school-success/homework-help/homework-project-tips/good-homework-habits.html

Cross, J. (2023, August 24). *What does too much screen time do to kids' brains?* New York Presbyterian. https://healthmatters.nyp.org/what-does-too-much-screen-time-do-to-childrens-brains/

Devine, M. (n.d.). *Empowering parents.* Empowering Parents. https://www.empoweringparents.com/article/screen-time-using-technology-as-a-consequence-or-reward-for-your-child/

Do babies get bored? Why a bored baby is a good thing. (n.d). Enfamil. https://www.enfamil.com/articles/do-babies-get-bored/

Durning, M. V. (n.d.). *Tolerance, physical dependence, and addiction explained.* WebMD. https://www.webmd.com/mental-health/addiction/tolerance-dependence-addiction-explained

Dzioba, H. (2021, October). *Setting boundaries – managing cyberbullying in the workplace.* SOS Safety Magazine. https://soskids.ca/uncategorized/setting-boundaries-managing-cyberbullying-in-the-workplace

Edmondson, R. (2018, May 8). *Screen time for small kids: education or entertainment?* Spokane County Library District. https://www.scld.org/screen-time-for-small-kids-education-or-entertainment/

Einstein, A. (n.d.). *A quote by Albert Einstein.* Goodreads. https://www.goodreads.com/quotes/7091-it-has-become-appallingly-obvious-that-our-technology-has-exceeded

Elaidam, R. P. (2024, January 25). *Raising kids without technology: Screen-Free childhood.* Medium. https://elaidamramesh.medium.com/raising-kids-without-technology-the-benefits-of-screen-free-living-cb444852ec83

Ellis, T. (2024, February 26). *The benefits of imaginative play.* Therapy Focus. https://therapyfocus.org.au/on-the-blog/the-benefits-of-imaginative-play/

The environment: Schedules and routines. (2012). Virtual Lab School. https://www.virtuallabschool.org/preschool/learning-environments/lesson-5

Erinna. (2022, November 23). *Modern-day parenting: How screen time affects your child's mental health.* Medical Health Associates of Western New York. https://www.mhawny.com/2022/11/23/modern-day-parenting-how-screen-time-affects-your-childs-mental-health/

Family media plan. (2019). Chapman University. https://bpb-us-w2.wpmucdn.com/sites.chapman.edu/dist/f/613/files/2019/07/Family-Media-Plan.pdf

Family media plans. (2014). Turning Life On. https://www.turninglifeon.org/family-media-plans

Feiler, B. (2013, December 31). *The secrets of happy families: Improve your mornings, tell your family history, fight smarter, go out and play, and much more.* William Morrow Paperbacks.

Fieldhouse, C. (2022, May 14). *Is your child A tech zombie? How to go screen free.* The Ethical List. https://theethicalist.com/child-screen-free/

Foss, S. (2023, March 10). *My 5-year-old's moderate screen time limits showed me I'm on my phone and computer too much.* Business Insider. https://www.businessinsider.com/how-parents-model-responsible-screen-time-for-their-children-2023-3

Garg, A. (2021, April 16). *Post-screen-time anger and frustration in kids.* Allina Health. https://www.allinahealth.org/healthysetgo/prevent/post-screen-time-anger-frustration-in-kids

Gates, B. (n.d.). *Bill Gates quotes.* BrainyQuote. https://www.brainyquote.com/quotes/bill_gates_390682?src=t_technology

Happiest Baby Staff. (n.d.). *Your baby's brain: Why the first 3 years matter so much.* Happiest Baby. https://www.happiestbaby.com/blogs/baby/baby-brain-development

Harguth, A. (2021, May 18). *Screen time and body weight — is there a connection?* Mayo Clinic Health System. https://www.mayoclinichealthsystem.org/hometown-health/speaking-of-health/screen-time-and-body-weight-is-there-a-connection

Harris, B. (n.d.). *A quote by Bonnie Harris.* In *Habyts Blog,* (2016, March 15). Scream time? Our 10 favourite screen time quotes and learnings. Habyts. https://habyts.com/scream-time-our-10-favourite-screen-time-quotes-and-learnings/

Harris, S. J. (n.d.). *Sydney J. Harris quotes.* BrainyQuote. https://www.brainyquote.com/quotes/sydney_j_harris _104631

Hartnett, J. K. (2022, March). *Delayed speech or language development.* KidsHealth. https://kidshealth.org/en/parents/not-talk.html

Hartung, E. (2018, October 10). *The 10 warning signs of cyberbullying.* Net Nanny. https://www.netnanny.com/blog/the-10-warning-signs-of-cyberbullying/

Healthy eating: Is too much screen time causing weight gain in children? (n.d.). Walden University. https://www.waldenu.edu/programs/health/resource/ is-too-much-screen-time-causing-weight-gain-in-children

Help your teen manage their social media usage. (n.d.). Reach Out Australia. https://parents.au.reachout.com/staying-safe-online/social-media/help-your-teen-manage-their-social-media-usage

Helping your child with time management: 5 gentle approach techniques. (2023, June 1). GT Scholars. https://gtscholars.org/helping-your-child-with-time-management-5-gentle-approach-techniques

Herrity, J. (2019, March 15). *Social skills: Definition and examples.* Indeed. https://www.indeed.com/career-advice/career-development/social-skills

Hill, D. (2016, October 21). *Why to avoid TV for infants and toddlers.* Healthy Children.

https://www.healthychildren.org/English/family-
life/Media/Pages/Why-to-Avoid-TV-Before-Age-
2.aspx

Hinduja, S., & Patchin, J. W. (2018, June 1). *What to do when your
child is cyberbullied: Top ten tips for parents*. Cyberbullying
Research Center. https://cyberbullying.org/what-to-
do-when-your-child-is-cyberbullied

Hovde, M. (2022, July 27). *ADHD and screen time: What's the
link?* Psych Central.
https://psychcentral.com/adhd/screen-time-and-
children-with-adhd

How does screen time affect your sleep? (2023, December 14). Integris
Health. https://integrishealth.org/resources/on-your-
health/2023/december/how-does-screen-time-affect-
your-sleep

How to build self-confidence in the digital age. (2023, July 14). Be Seen.
https://www.beseenhub.com/lifestyle-and-
wellness/smile-confidence/boost-self-confidence-in-
the-digital-age/

Hunter, B. (2015, July 21). *Easy no-fuss screen time reward system*.
Home Stories A to Z.
https://www.homestoriesatoz.com/tips-2/easy-no-
fuss-screen-time-reward-system.html

The importance of schedules and routines. (2024, July 23). Early
Childhood Learning & Knowledge Center.
https://eclkc.ohs.acf.hhs.gov/quienes-
somos/articulo/importance-schedules-routines

Infante, M. (2024, February 11). *Ten activities for baby to boost bonding and development.* Babies and Bumps. https://babies-and-bumps.com/resources/10-activities-for-baby-to-boost-bonding-development/

Is screen time hurting your back and neck? (n.d.). Stretch Zone. https://www.stretchzone.com/blog-posts/is-screen-time-hurting-your-back-and-neck

jazzpunkcommathe. (2023, November). *Is this generation of kids truly less engaged/intellectually curious compared to previous generations?* Reddit. https://www.reddit.com/r/Teachers/comments/180x 1to/is_this_generation_of_kids_truly_less/

Jenkins, J. S. (2001). The Mozart Effect. *Journal of the Royal Society of Medicine, 94*(4), 170–172. https://doi.org/10.1177/014107680109400404

Johnson, A. (2022, March 9). *Screen time recommendations by age.* All about Vision. https://www.allaboutvision.com/conditions/refractive-errors/screen-time-by-age/

Johnson, C. A. (2015, August 25). *A quote by Clay A. Johnson.* In *The information diet: A case for curious consumption.* O'Reilly Media.

Kattoor, S. (2023, December 13). *Time management for teens made easy in 5 steps: Parents guide.* Rise Crimson Education. https://rise.crimsoneducation.org/articles/time-management-for-teens-made-easy-in-5-steps-parents-guide

Keer, H. (2024). *How to keep the kids engaged home during free time.* Aditya Birla World Academy. https://www.adityabirlaworldacademy.com/blog/how-to-keep-the-kids-engaged-home-during-free-time

Kids & music: Effects of music on child development. (2018, May 23). School of Rock. https://www.schoolofrock.com/resources/music-education/kids-music-effects-of-music-on-child-development

King, E. W. (2022, December 14). *Teaching kids to manage free time.* Learn with Dr. Emily. https://learnwithdremily.substack.com/p/teaching-kids-to-manage-free-time

Lange, C. L. (n.d.). *Christian Lous Lange quotes.* BrainyQuote. https://www.brainyquote.com/quotes/christian_lous_lange_335254

Lawrenson, E. (2024, August 6). *Five tips to help balance screen time and learning.* Qustodio. https://www.qustodio.com/en/blog/tips-to-balance-screen-time-and-learning/

Li, J., Huang, Z., Si, W., & Shao, T. (2022). The effects of physical activity on positive emotions in children and adolescents: A systematic review and meta-analysis. *International Journal of Environmental Research and Public Health, 19*(21), 14185. https://doi.org/10.3390/ijerph192114185

Lillard, A. S., & Peterson, J. (2011). The immediate impact of different types of television on young children's executive function. *Pediatrics*, *128*(4), 644–649. https://doi.org/10.1542/peds.2010-1919

Littman, E. (2024, August 21). *Never enough? Why ADHD brains crave stimulation.* ADDitude. https://www.additudemag.com/brain-stimulation-and-adhd-cravings-dependency-and-regulation/

Making, tinkering and the benefits of hands-on play. (2021, February 22). Heart-Mind Online. https://heartmindonline.org/resources/making-tinkering-and-the-benefits-of-hands-on-play

Malik, A. (2021, December 20). *How too much screen time affects kids' eyes: Tips to prevent eye strain.* Children's Hospital of Philadelphia. https://www.chop.edu/news/health-tip/how-too-much-screen-time-affects-kids-eyes

Mayo Clinic Staff. (2024, January 18). *Teens and social media use: What's the impact?* Mayo Clinic. https://www.mayoclinic.org/healthy-lifestyle/tween-and-teen-health/in-depth/teens-and-social-media-use/art-20474437

McNulty, C. (2022, March 231). *My son's story of electronics addiction and recovery.* ADDitude. https://www.additudemag.com/video-game-addiction-digital-detox/

Mimi. (2021, May 30). *No screen time for baby under 2 - how to deal.* Indulge with Bibi. https://www.indulgewithbibi.com/no-screen-time-for-baby-under-2-how-to-deal/

Mokhonoana, M. (n.d.). *Mokokoma Mokhonoana quotes.* Goodreads. https://www.goodreads.com/quotes/7440298-people-who-smile-while-they-are-alone-used-to-be

Moreno, M. (2024, February 12). *Why co-viewing is important: Tips to share screen time with your kids.* HealthyChildren. https://www.healthychildren.org/English/family-life/Media/Pages/why-co-viewing-is-important-tips-to-share-screen-time-with-your-kids.aspx

Morgan-Richards, L. (2017). *Lorin Morgan-Richards quotes.* Goodreads. https://www.goodreads.com/quotes/8889688-old-robots-are-becoming-more-human-and-young-humans-are

Myers, P. (2013, May 6). *Hobbies are healthy.* Child Development Info. https://childdevelopmentinfo.com/child-activities/hobbies-are-healthy/

Nagata, J. M., Chu, J., Ganson, K. T., Murray, S. B., Iyer, P., Gabriel, K. P., Garber, A. K., Bibbins-Domingo, K., & Baker, F. C. (2022). Contemporary screen time modalities and disruptive behavior disorders in children: A prospective cohort study. *Journal of Child Psychology and Psychiatry, 64*(1), 125-135. https://doi.org/10.1111/jcpp.13673

Nagel, M. C., & Sharman, R. (2022, April 30). *Becoming autistic: How technology is altering the minds of the next generation.* Amba Press.

Nagel, M., & Sharman, R. (2023, September 21). *Excessive screen time can affect young people's emotional development.* The Conversation. https://theconversation.com/excessive-screen-time-can-affect-young-peoples-emotional-development-213869

Naskar, A. (2015). *Abhijit Naskar quotes.* Goodreads. https://www.goodreads.com/quotes/10906456-smartwatches-don-t-keep-you-fit-activity-does-do-you-really

Nelson, C. (n.d.). *Babies need humans, not screens.* UNICEF Parenting. https://www.unicef.org/parenting/child-development/babies-screen-time

Nguyen, L. (2023, January 9). *What you need to know about the relationship between screen time and ADHD.* Foothills Academy. https://www.foothillsacademy.org/community/articles/what-you-need-to-know

O'Conner, K. (2019, August 23). *Schedules vs. free playtime: How to help kids find the balance.* Center for Children and Youth. https://ccy.jfcs.org/schedules-vs-free-playtime-help-kids-find-balance/

Otsuka, T. (2024, June 11). How to break the exhausting habit of revenge bedtime procrastination. *ADDitude.* https://www.additudemag.com/revenge-bedtime-procrastination-sleep-problems-adhd/

Our family media plan. (2022, January). Institute of Child Psychology.

https://instituteofchildpsychology.com/wp-content/uploads/2022/01/Family-Media-plan-1.pdf

Overby, E. (2018). *Eric Overby quotes.* Goodreads. https://www.goodreads.com/quotes/9118319-be-present-to-the-people-in-front-of-you-from

Pacheco, D. (2021, January 15). *Perfecting your child's bedtime routine.* Sleep Foundation. https://www.sleepfoundation.org/children-and-sleep/bedtime-routine

Pacheco, D., & Vyas, N. (2023, March 14). *Screen time and insomnia: What it means for teens.* Sleep Foundation. https://www.sleepfoundation.org/teens-and-sleep/screen-time-and-insomnia-for-teens

Parents and screen time: role-modelling for children. (2022, October 11). Raising Children Network. https://raisingchildren.net.au/grown-ups/family-life/media-technology/parent-technology-use

Parlakian, R. (2016, February 1). *How to help your child develop empathy.* Zero to Three. https://www.zerotothree.org/resource/how-to-help-your-child-develop-empathy/

Pelchen, L. (2024, March 1). *Internet usage statistics in 2024.* Forbes Home. https://www.forbes.com/home-improvement/internet/internet-statistics/

Pope Paul VI. (n.d.). *Pope Paul VI quotes.* BrainyQuote. https://www.brainyquote.com/quotes/pope_paul_vi_390685?src=t_technology

Price, C. (2018). *Catherine Price quotes*. Goodreads. https://www.goodreads.com/quotes/10157723-this-is-a-really-big-deal-because-our-attention-is

Price, C. (2018, January 8). *Strengthening your teen's social and conversation abilities*. Hey Sigmund. https://www.heysigmund.com/strengthening-teens-social-conversation-abilities/

Robinson, S. (2024, June). *What is technology addiction (internet addiction)?* TechTarget. https://www.techtarget.com/searchcio/definition/Internet-addiction

Rosenblatt, J. (2019, April 17). More screen time linked to higher risk of ADHD in preschool-aged children: Study. *ABC News*. https://abcnews.go.com/Health/screen-time-linked-higher-risk-adhd-preschool-aged/story?id=62429157

Saline, S. (2021, April 26). *How much screen time for kids with ADHD is too much?* ADDitude. https://www.additudemag.com/how-much-screen-time-for-kids-adhd/

Sato, K. (2024, March 22). *Researcher says high screen time associated with social, emotional problems in children*. ABC News. https://www.abc.net.au/news/2024-03-22/research-finds-screen-time-video-games-linked-social-problems/103606100

Schaar, J. H. (n.d). *J. H. Schaar quotes*. Goodreads. https://www.goodreads.com/quotes/279924-the-future-is-not-some-place-we-are-going-but

Screen time and its impact on mental health and brain development- what can forbrain do? (n.d.). Forbrain. https://blog.forbrain.com/blog/screen-time-mental-health-brain-development-forbrain

Setting screen time limits for a balanced family life–learning made personal. (2023, November 9). School Pen. https://parents.schoolpen.net/setting-screen-time-limits-for-a-balanced-family-life/

Sheldon-Dean, H. (2020). *Screen time during the coronavirus crisis.* Child Mind Institute. https://childmind.org/article/screen-time-during-the-coronavirus-crisis/

Sriram, R. (2020, June 24). *Why ages 2-7 matter so much for brain development.* Edutopia. https://www.edutopia.org/article/why-ages-2-7-matter-so-much-brain-development/

Sternlicht, L., & Sternlicht, A. (n.d.). *The 6 most common types of technology addiction: Family addiction specialist.* Family Addiction Specialist. https://www.familyaddictionspecialist.com/blog/the-6-most-common-types-of-technology-addiction

Straker, L., & Zabatiero, J. (2024, February 21). *Using screens can affect a child's physical health and development, but that doesn't mean screens are bad.* ABC Education. https://www.abc.net.au/education/how-screens-affect-physical-health-and-development-of-children/103215644

Susman, C. (2020). *How to crush screen overuse with ADHD*. Cheryl Susman. https://cherylsusman.com/collected-wisdom/how-to-crush-screen-overuse-with-adhd

Sylvestro, D., & Kessler, E. (2016). *Promote social skills: Step away from the screen*. Smart Kids with Learning Disabilities. https://www.smartkidswithld.org/getting-help/making-friends/promote-social-skills-step-away-screen/

Takahashi, I., Obara, T., Ishikuro, M., Murakami, K., Ueno, F., Noda, A., Onuma, T., Shinoda, G., Nishimura, T., Tsuchiya, K. J., & Kuriyama, S. (2023). Screen time at age 1 year and communication and problem-solving developmental delay at 2 and 4 years. *JAMA Pediatrics*, *177*(10), 1039–1046. https://doi.org/10.1001/jamapediatrics.2023.3057

Taleb, N. N. (n.d.). *Nassim Nicholas Taleb quotes*. Goodreads. https://www.goodreads.com/quotes/610831-every-social-association-that-is-not-face-to-face-is-injurious-to

Taylor, & Francis. (2023, November 17). *Children's brains shaped by their time on tech devices, research to-date shows*. Newswise. https://d.newswise.com/articles/children-s-brains-shaped-by-their-time-on-tech-devices-research-to-date-shows

Tips on how to help your kids do their homework correctly! (2024, March 5). 21K School South Africa. https://www.21kschool.com/za/blog/tips-to-help-kids-do-their-homework-correctly/

Toffler, A. (n.d.). *Alvin Toffler quotes*. Goodreads. https://www.goodreads.com/quotes/8800-the-illiterate-of-the-21st-century-will-not-be-those

Too much screen time? - 4 signs to watch for in your child. (2018, December 13). Center for Mental Wellness. https://socalmentalwellness.com/child-counseling/too-much-screen-time/

Tritsch, E. (2022, January 1). *How to set goals for teens - the SMART goals method.* Fairborn Digital Academy. https://fairborndigital.us/2022/01/01/smart-goals-for-teens/

Twenge, J. M., & Campbell, W. K. (2018). Associations between screen time and lower psychological well-being among children and adolescents: Evidence from a population-based study. *Preventive Medicine Reports, 12*(12), 271–283. https://doi.org/10.1016/j.pmedr.2018.10.003

Van Hoof, K. (2023, July 11). *Five best apps for limiting screen time in 2024: No loopholes.* Safety Detectives. https://www.safetydetectives.com/blog/best-apps-for-limiting-screen-time/

VanOrman, A. (2022, August 8). *Anxiety and depression increase among U.S. youth, 2022 KIDS COUNTS data book shows.* Population Reference Bureau. https://www.prb.org/resources/anxiety-and-depression-increase-among-u-s-youth-2022-kids-counts-data-book-shows/

Vogels, E. (2022, December 15). *Teens and cyberbullying 2022.* Pew Research Center. https://www.pewresearch.org/internet/2022/12/15/teens-and-cyberbullying-2022/

Waghorn, E. (2024, July 27). *Tips to managing family screen time fairly.* Daily Maverick. https://www.dailymaverick.co.za/article/2024-07-27-tips-to-managing-family-screen-time-fairly/

What to do if your child is a bully. (n.d.). Stomp Out Bullying. https://www.stompoutbullying.org/what-do-if-your-child-bully

Wine, T. (2021). *Thatcher Wine quotes.* Goodreads. https://www.goodreads.com/quotes/11028112-if-your-family-has-gotten-used-to-having-devices-at

Wright, L. W. (n.d.). *Types of social cues.* Understood. https://www.understood.org/en/articles/4-types-of-social-cues

World Health Organization. (n.d.). *Mental health.* https://www.who.int/health-topics/mental-health

Yunus, M. (n.d.). *Muhammad Yunus quotes.* BrainyQuote. https://www.brainyquote.com/quotes/muhammad_yunus_593352?src=t_technology

Zapal, H. (2024, June 13). *How to model healthy screen time habits for your kids.* Bark. https://www.bark.us/blog/healthy-screen-time-habits/

Image References

Cottonbro Studio. (2021a). Photograph of a family looking at a photo album [Image]. *Pexels*. https://www.pexels.com/photo/photograph-of-a-family-looking-at-a-photo-album-6667307/

Cottonbro Studio. (2021b). Young boy wearing jumper painting on a paper [Image]. *Pexels*. https://www.pexels.com/photo/young-boy-wearing-jumper-painting-on-a-paper-7898617/

Fortunato, W. (2020). Young diverse students having coffee break in street cafe [Image]. *Pexels*. https://www.pexels.com/photo/young-diverse-students-having-coffee-break-in-street-cafe-6140366/

IMG_1979 Ševonka. (2019). Photo of women playing basketball [Image]. *Pexels*. https://www.pexels.com/photo/photo-of-women-playing-basketball-3425993/

Kampus Production. (2021). Man in white crew neck t-shirt holding fork and eating [Image]. *Pexels*. https://www.pexels.com/photo/man-in-white-crew-neck-t-shirt-holding-fork-and-eating-7492949/

Lach, R. (2021). Mother and son stretching on jetty [Image]. *Pexels*. https://www.pexels.com/photo/mother-and-son-stretching-on-jetty-9963957/

Lewis, J. (2020). Children lying on sofa and using gadgets [Image]. *Pexels*.

https://www.pexels.com/photo/children-lying-on-sofa-and-using-gadgets-4200824/

Lopes, H. (2020). Young man writing reminder on fridge note [Image]. *Pexels.* https://www.pexels.com/photo/young-man-writing-reminder-on-fridge-note-3866999/

Lopes, H. (2022). Son and mother watching TV together while sitting on couch [Image]. *Pexels.* https://www.pexels.com/photo/son-and-mother-watching-tv-together-while-sitting-on-couch-11589680/

Podrez, A. (2021). Two kids doing some artworks [Image]. *Pexels.* https://www.pexels.com/photo/two-kids-doing-some-artworks-6941092/

RDNE Stock Project. (2020). Close-up shot of a person sending text message [Image]. *Pexels.* https://www.pexels.com/photo/close-up-shot-of-a-person-sending-text-message-4921407/

RDNE Stock Project. (2021). Girls wearing sportwear standing by the tennis net [Image]. *Pexels.* https://www.pexels.com/photo/girls-wearing-sportswear-standing-by-the-tennis-net-8224718/

RDNE Stock Project. (2021). Woman writing in calendar [Image]. *Pexels.* https://www.pexels.com/photo/woman-writing-in-calendar-8581118/

Samkov, I. (2021). Baby boy playing with wooden toy on floor [Image]. *Pexels.* https://www.pexels.com/photo/baby-boy-playing-with-wooden-toy-on-floor-8504336/

Shvets, A. (2022). A family sitting together in a living room [Image]. *Pexels.* https://www.pexels.com/photo/a-family-sitting-together-in-a-living-room-11368546/

Smith, J. M. (2017). Man wearing green printed crew neck shirt while sleeping [Image]. *Pexels.* https://www.pexels.com/photo/man-wearing-green-printed-crew-neck-shirt-while-sleeping-296817/

Subiyanto, K. (2020). Positive ethnic mother and little children choosing TV channel together [Image]. *Pexels.* https://www.pexels.com/photo/positive-ethnic-mother-and-little-children-choosing-tv-channel-together-4474003/

Made in the USA
Monee, IL
27 November 2024

71396812R00125